THE HORSE RIDER'S
PROBLEM SOLVER

THE HORSE RIDER'S PROBLEM SOLVER

Provides practical solutions to the most common problems relating to riding and schooling

VANESSA BRITTON

DAVID & CHARLES

CONTENTS

PART 1 The Young Horse 11

PART 2 Schooling 49

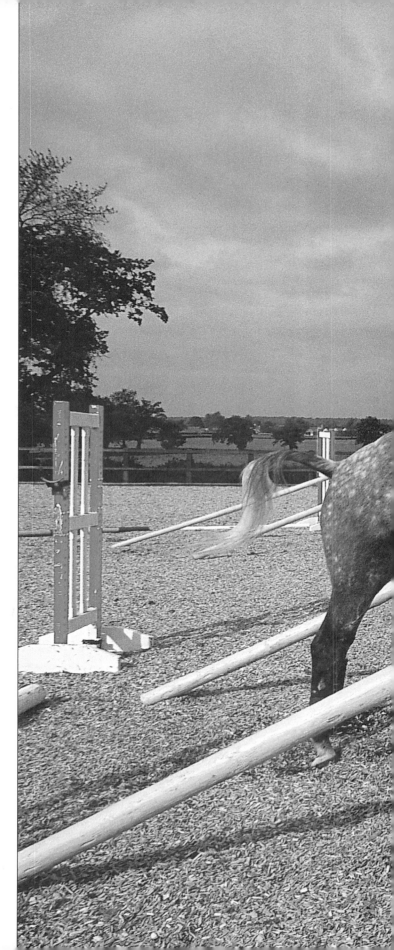

All photographs by Vanessa Britton except pp2, 8–9, 28, 29, 58 (right), 81, 121, 122, 138, 139 and 145 by Kit Houghton; pp16 (btm left) and p133 (top) Bob Langrish; pp44 and 147 Your Horse magazine; p106 Stephen Sparkes and p117 Sue Williams-Gardner

Line illustrations: pp26, 29 and 126 by Sally Alexander; pp15, 78 and 79 Monty Mortimer; p97 Paul Bale and pp110–11 Eva Melhuish

A DAVID & CHARLES BOOK

First published in the UK in 1997

A catalogue record for this book is available from the British Library.

ISBN 0 7153 0613 8

Printed in the UK by Caledonian International Book Manufacturing Ltd for David & Charles
Brunel House   Newton Abbot   Devon

Part 1:
THE YOUNG

HORSE

Learning to trust

PROBLEM The key to a successful relationship when training a young horse is gaining his trust. How can this be achieved?

SOLUTION The young horse must always be treated as an individual, and with respect, in the same way as one would bring up a child. When training a young horse it may help to remember that what is put into the relationship will be returned at a later date. Also, it is generally easier to build up a good relationship if the horse has been handled by the same person, so he learns to recognise certain commands and does not become confused. The horse which respects his trainer does not fear him; and he will learn respect through trust, familiar and reassuring surroundings, and regularity. A timid and frightened youngster may take a long while to realise that a new handler and potential leader is not a threat; in this case owners may find that spending time in the field or stable and talking to him works wonders.

Once the initial bond has been established, it is important to teach the horse discipline. Throughout his training he will be required to concentrate and to do what he is asked, and must accept there is a time for work and a time for play. Discipline is not a question of bullying the horse into submission, it is about laying down certain rules which will apply throughout his training. Titbits can prove useful when disciplining youngsters, as food is constantly on their mind. However, while a carrot can serve as a special treat for good behaviour, verbal praise is often more beneficial when combined with an encouraging pat.

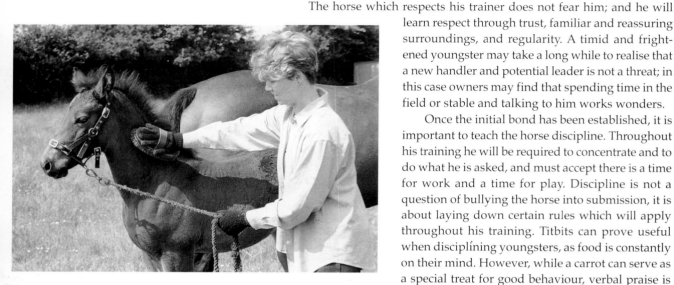

It is much wiser to handle the young foal and not let it just run wild; in a few quiet lessons you should be able to teach him to lead, to have his legs and feet handled and picked up, and to be brushed on his tickly parts, and by establishing mutual understanding and respect at an early age he will find it much easier to accept his later education.

All trainers have different ideas on chastisement, and the amount given will depend on the individual horse. A sharp 'No' will often suffice for a small misdemeanour, but a smack may be necessary for nastiness. Of course, it is very important to chastise immediately so the horse relates the punishment to what he has just done. Most young horses are quite willing to co-operate; however, some may need a little extra telling off – although this should never amount to the handler losing his temper or using unnecessary force. Ultimately the amount of disciplining given should be left to an experienced person's discretion.

BEHAVIOURAL PROBLEMS

Anyone who encounters behavioural problems with their youngster should seek knowledgeable help, as one wrong move when disciplining can lead to problems later in the horse's life. Many of the problems discussed in Part Two can be traced to the horse's initial training, and have perhaps arisen because of a lack of trust or respect on the part of both horse and rider. Establishing a solid relationship during the horse's early years will undoubtedly reap benefits later on.

A good start

SOLUTION First of all you must realise that there are simply no hard and fast rules. Each horse is an individual and must be treated as such, and some horses will progress quickly, others more slowly. The most important aspect to appreciate is that regardless of time, the aim is to produce a horse with a good basic education; from this foundation he can be trained further in more specialised disciplines if desired. Lungeing is an excellent activity for youngsters as it helps to improve their manners and confidence, while the handler can see what is happening.

1   It is essential that the going under foot is good.
2   The horse should be made to move well forwards and up to the bit, the handler's voice encouraging him, with a flick of the lungeing whip if necessary; the use of elasticated side-reins will help him to balance himself, and teach him the correct feel of the rein.
3   The main objective is to encourage him to move actively forwards in a good, balanced rhythm.
4   Side-reins are best used at trot to begin with: the movement of the horse's head is considerably more in walk, and unless the person lungeing is experienced, side-reins fitted and used incorrectly could upset the rhythm of the pace.
5   Once the horse is moving freely forwards in each pace on the lunge, the work can be repeated under saddle. (More help is given for specific problems throughout this chapter.)

PROBLEM Having bought a young, recently backed horse of three or four years old, most people are very anxious to do everything right in order not to 'spoil' it. What is the best way forwards, and how long should it take to school a young horse?

Lungeing correctly is a great skill, and much can be learned from watching and listening to those who are proficient at it. Gaining some practical experience with horses which have been taught to lunge correctly will be of immense benefit when it comes to lungeing inexperienced youngsters.

Water shyness

PROBLEM Many young horses seem to have an intrinsic dislike of water, and this can lead them to refuse to walk through puddles or streams when out hacking. Such a phobia could prove dangerous, as a horse may step sideways into the path of an overtaking or oncoming vehicle just to avoid getting his feet wet. How can this aversion to water be overcome?

SOLUTION Persuading a horse not to object to water requires a great deal of patience. With a young horse you are starting with a clean slate, and provided you go about his water training in a methodical and unhurried way, you can overcome for good any fear of water he might have. Older horses that have been frightened in some way will take a little longer, but the same principles apply.

A small puddle is the ideal starting-point, progressing to a small stream or shallow pool when the horse is ready. Once he has overcome his fear of water, it should be quite easy to train him to accept jumping into water during a cross-country round, or jumping over water when he is showjumping, if and when he needs to.

Do not choose a cold day to begin water training, because the horse will then associate splashing with cold discomfort. Choose a warm day after a hard ride when he will be more likely to associate water and splashing with cooling down, he will welcome this if he is hot and sticky.

1   In order to gain a horse's confidence you must set about persuading him that there is really nothing to fear, and as young horses learn by example, the best way of convincing him is for an older schoolmaster to offer a lead. This horse should have no qualms whatsoever about striding straight into and through a puddle or small stream, because a youngster will 'pick up' on any hesitation, however slight this might be.

2   The youngster should be made to walk right up close to the older horse's tail and encouraged strongly to step into the water. He may want to sniff the water first, which he should be allowed to do, but go through it he must. This can be done in hand at home, or while out hacking, depending on which situation offers the handler/rider most control.

3   As soon as the horse takes a step into the water he should be praised and offered a reward. Patience is the key. It may take some time just to persuade the horse to put one foot in – but if he is harassed he will begin to dislike water even further.

4   Should he stop dead when asked to step into the water he should not be hit or kicked vigorously, although every effort should be made to prevent him from stepping backwards. Often he will become bored and decide to go forwards of his own accord in order to join his companion.

Frightened of the lungeing whip

CAUSE   Some particularly nervous horses may always be a little frightened of the lunge whip, as it can move suddenly and they may associate it with pain, however slight. In some ways this is a good thing, as it is often easier to teach a timid horse not to fear the whip, than to re-train a bold and bolshy horse which does not respect it. The horse's initial handling may be the cause of this problem, as a handler who is careless and clumsy may make sudden movements which scare the horse and cause him to be jumpy.

PROBLEM   Some young horses find the lunge whip frightening or threatening, and they will shy away from it, rather than respect it. How can trainers teach the basics of lungeing without scaring the horse into submission?

SOLUTION   All youngsters should be handled quietly and calmly so they learn to take everything in their stride; if the handler is careful to do this throughout the training programme, new pieces of equipment or school movements may not seem so alarming.

The trainer must be sure he handles the whip carefully, and should not allow it to drag on the ground; if he does, the tail end may catch around clumps of grass or earth, then spring up like a catapult and scare the horse. When not in use, the whip should either be secured under the trainer's arm, pointing away from the horse's body, or if he is sure he can keep it still, he may hold it in his outside hand so it follows the horse's quarters, although it should be close to the ground and not swinging or cracking.

If the horse is genuinely scared the handler will need to use a schooling or dressage whip for lungeing, which is shorter and more rigid. Meanwhile the lunge whip may be introduced to other aspects of the horse's life, for instance while he is eating his tea. Or the handler may bring the horse out of his stable and hold the whip close by so the horse associates it with pleasant things, and not fear. Once the horse is accustomed to the lunge whip in his everyday life, it may take the place of the schooling whip during the lungeing sessions. The handler must be careful to keep the whip still at all times, and use a calming voice to reassure the horse.

It may be useful for the horse to be lunged with a rider, the handler using the whip and the rider reassuring the horse and preventing him from speeding up.

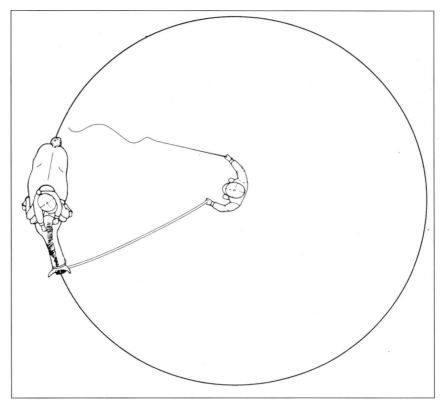

The lunge whip has two main uses: to keep the horse out on a circle, and to encourage him to work with impulsion from the quarters. Once he has overcome his fear he will probably lunge quite nicely, as he will be willing to move away from the whip when asked, but without panic.

Excitable on the lunge

PROBLEM Some horses refuse to work calmly on the lunge, running faster on the circle and leaning in or 'motorbiking'. How can they be calmed down and encouraged to concentrate on the job in hand?

CAUSE There are two main reasons for a horse getting excited and misbehaving on the lunge: either he is in pain, and is finding what is being asked of him too difficult; or he is generally excitable and misbehaves in other areas, too. The reason some horses are obviously in discomfort on the lunge rather than when they are being schooled or led in hand, is because the circle is so tight, and because they have to balance and use the quarters. Lungeing is actually difficult for the young horse, particularly at first when he is still undeveloped and immature. The fault may lie with the handler, as most people are taught to pivot in one spot and let the horse move around them on a twenty-metre circle. A young horse may find it difficult to take in all the instructions he is given anyway, and is bound to find maintaining a perfect circle impossible; the handler should therefore move round in a small circle as well, so that he is not asking too much of the horse.

If the horse is in pain he will undoubtedly try to evade it, which may cause him to speed up or to lean in. Alternatively the lungeing he is being asked to do may simply be too difficult for him; or he could be suffering from a physical problem. Any weakness in the body which adversely affects the horse's weight-carrying ability may cause evasion, so owners should have him examined by a veterinary surgeon or a back specialist if they are concerned.

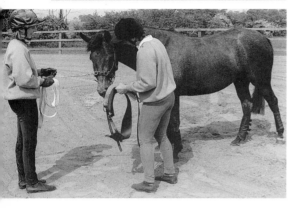

Rather than marching up to your horse and slapping on the roller straightaway, which will almost certainly give him a fright, show it to him first and let him sniff it.

(below left) A single-ring, three-strap cavesson and (right) a three-ring cavesson

SOLUTION If the horse is merely excited and naturally high-spirited, it is a matter of calming him down and establishing the difference between work and play; once he relaxes, his speed should decrease, which in turn will mean his balance will improve. There is nothing to be gained from just rushing around for twenty minutes. First the horse must learn to walk quietly in hand: the trainer should therefore tack him up as if for lungeing, but then lead him round the schooling area on a large circle. Transitions through halt and walk should help, the handler using firm voice aids and carrying a short whip; this may be used to tap the horse on the shoulder should he try and walk forwards in impatience.

Once the horse has accomplished this with the han-

dler at his shoulder, the lunge line may be lengthened to about arms' length and the exercise repeated. This may take some time, as the handler will not be able to restrain the horse physically – it must be walking and halting in response to the handler's voice alone. A light tweak on the lunge line may encourage a halt, the horse being praised when he behaves correctly. This exercise should be repeated, with the lunge line increasing in length each time; the handler must walk a large circle himself so the exercise does not become too difficult for the horse. The horse must be totally competent and responsive in walk before any other gait is attempted, as this may encourage him to speed up once more. There is no rush after all; even if the horse takes weeks or months to walk quietly on a circle it will be worthwhile in the end.

Trot work should be introduced gradually with just a few steps each time, the horse re-balancing the walk before going forwards into trot once more. If he has been backed, the added weight of a rider as he is being worked may slow him down. If not, it is just a matter of gaining his respect, and of taking the time to educate him properly.

Dressed and ready for lungeing, with protective boots all round and a pad under the roller to prevent chafing. If the horse knocks into himself, or the pressure of the roller makes him sore, he could very quickly become upset; note, too, the reins taken through the throatlash and twisted under the gullet to prevent them flapping about and frightening him.

Calming herbs and supplements may help to relax a horse. However, take care to feed the correct dose, because some chemicals or minerals may cause an imbalance in the diet, and can even impede a young horse's growth.

Inattention on the lunge

PROBLEM Youngsters are renowned for their short attention span and inquisitiveness. How can the horse's inquiring mind be adapted so that he concentrates whilst on the lunge?

SOLUTION Where new experiences are concerned, young horses are notoriously excitable, and quite lacking in concentration until they have adapted to their new environment. Unfortunately this may lead to inattentiveness whilst lungeing or schooling, which in turn may lead to excitement or bad behaviour. Fortunately the horse's natural inquisitiveness can very often be used to advantage, as intelligent horses are quick to learn and generally very willing. The young horse's lifestyle should be varied and interesting, though with a sense of regularity and routine; he should also be well handled and respectful of his trainer, who should always insist that he pays attention to the commands he is given.

Various devices and 'passe-temps' may be provided, to help ease boredom and to put the horse's mind to good use; for instance a resilient rubber ball to play with in the field or stable.

The trainer should establish a set of regular commands for use when lungeing, so the horse learns what is required through association. Later on, when he is ridden, the commands will be used again so that he can associate the rider's verbal instructions with the aids applied simultaneously. As the horse does not recognise words as such, the tone of the command is important. For instance, when asking him to go forwards into an upward transition, the latter half of the word should be encouraging and in an upward tone; whereas for a downward transition, the latter half should be in a lower tone, said in a soothing manner. The horse will learn to recognise the commands through their tone, and will also get to know whether the trainer is pleased and encouraging, or chastising and firm. Examples of commands are 'walk on', 'ter-rott', and 'can-ter'; and 'wa-alk', as in 'wo-oah'. Also useful are terms such as 'no' for chastising, 'good boy' for praise, and 'out' for encouraging the horse to walk to the outer circle.

The key to maintaining the horse's attention is to keep the training session varied, so include frequent transitions and several changes of rein. Clicking with the tongue will keep him listening, as will a gentle flick with the lunge whip. Outside distractions such as other horses or yard activity should be kept to a minimum, so the horse's eye is not caught by something apparently more interesting. It may also help to fit a fly fringe with ears, as this will reduce additional noise such as wind and voices.

Of course there is nothing wrong with natural exuberance or inquisitiveness, providing the horse's trainer can channel it usefully and capitalise on it during the schooling process.

The more variety the better for young horses, including kicking a ball about the yard! Left for hours in a stable with nothing to do, they are almost bound to mess about and be inattentive when you do take them out – so keep them occupied, amused and busy as much as possible!

Circling on the lunge: 1

SOLUTION It is to be expected that the young horse will want to come in to his handler – he probably walks towards him in the field, and is almost certainly not used to being asked to walk away from him. However, most youngsters do learn what is required quite quickly, provided lungeing is a natural progression from handling and leading in hand. By the time the horse is considered ready to lunge he should have learnt to halt when asked, to turn away from the handler, and to walk quietly at his shoulder. At this early stage a lunge cavesson is most suitable; only when his education is more advanced should the lunge line be attached to the bit. It will be beneficial to lead the horse in hand whilst wearing the cavesson to begin with, so he becomes accustomed to the rings and the feeling of the contact.

PROBLEM The lungeing process may be confusing for young horses, often causing some to keep turning in when they should be keeping on the circle. How can this situation be remedied calmly and effectively?

It can be very dangerous for the horse to turn in on the circle, as the lunge line may get caught up around his legs if the handler cannot gather it up in time. This is not a serious problem if the horse is docile and content to walk, but some more excitable horses may trot and then begin to panic. If the problem is not addressed early on in life, it can develop into a nasty habit, the horse coming into the centre and running the handler over or trying to bite him. This is obviously an extreme reaction, but one which the author has personally witnessed as a result of careless training when the horse was young.

Careful use of the lunge whip may also be helpful: point it at the horse's shoulder, and as long as he respects the whip he will not feel scared or threatened by this, but will keep to the outside.

It will help enormously to have an additional handler on the horse's outside, so that he follows the line of the circle; thus if he attempts to turn in, the handler can lead him back to the outside. Even once he has apparently learned to keep to the outside of the circle, it may be wise to have the assistant there should the horse lose concentration and drift inwards.

The handler should have a series of commands for use when lungeing, for instance, 'wa-alk', 'ter-ott', 'can-ter'. As discussed in 'Inattention on the Lunge', the commands requiring an upward transition should finish on an upbeat note and be quite enthusiastic, whereas the commands for a downward transition should be calm and soothing. It may help to have a command for 'out', which is quite firm and authoritative; this can be used in conjunction with the lunge whip and is usually quite effective.

Circling on the lunge: 2

PROBLEM Conversely, some horses may try to pull to the outside of the circle. How can this be prevented?

SOLUTION Although not as common as turning in, this is still serious as it may lead to the handler being dragged. The horse which pulls to the outside of the circle is in danger of developing a very hard mouth, and may also prove stiff and unyielding. As a result, the handler may be tempted to give short tugs to encourage the horse into the circle again, but this will lead to it ignoring the sensation or becoming more insolent.

The correct course of action is for the handler to make sure he is properly 'anchored', ie has a firm footing, is using his weight to his advantage and is positioned at an angle of 45° to the horse's head. The handler should not lean against the horse's contact, but should encourage him forwards firmly using the voice and lunge whip, keeping a fluid inside hand on the lunge rein. The horse should learn to work into the contact, so the handler must provide a consistent feel, as if he were riding. Working in a small enclosed area, perhaps by fencing off a section of the schooling arena, will help to combat this problem, and it will also reduce the possibility of the horse becoming distracted.

The correct position for the handler to stand in relation to the horse: basically this 'triangle' of handler/horse/lunge whip should be maintained at all paces, although the handler may need to move slightly behind the horse in order to move him more forwards if he is being sluggish, or slightly in front of him to slow him down.

Unwilling on the lunge

SOLUTION Fortunately this can be rectified with firm schooling. The handler must maintain impulsion from behind the horse, using the lunge whip and voice to encourage him forwards. In this instance the handler will need to move around the school himself, so that he gets closer to the horse's rear.

PROBLEM A horse which is just not keen to move forwards at all on the lunge is usually either 'bone idle' or simply inexperienced. How can he be encouraged to work properly?

The totally green horse may need to be led round the circle first by an assistant until he gets the idea of what is wanted. If he already 'knows the drill', however, and is being patently bolshy or lazy, more drastic action can be taken so that he does learn to go forwards when asked but don't let it turn into a circus act!

The handler is almost long-reining the horse, pushing from behind so that it really gets the idea of moving forwards into the contact. This may also be achieved by an assistant using a shorter whip and 'chasing the horse up' from behind. The purpose is not to scare the horse, but to make him use his hocks and gain the necessary impulsion and rhythm.

LUNGEING TIPS and PROBLEM SOLVER

■ *Patience and concentration are vital, and it is best to work in a secluded place so the horse is attentive to you.*

■ *To ensure the horse goes freely forwards and thereby establishes rhythm and balance – the aim of all training – stand at roughly 45° to his forehand and concentrate on the movement of his quarters rather than his head and back ie with your back slightly towards the horse's direction of travel.*

■ *If you are in control, the horse may be allowed a buck and a kick at the start of a lesson: this may well forestall later evasions.*

■ *Never use the side-reins to force a horse's head into position: rather, encourage him to*

lower his head and seek a contact with the bit by co-ordinating the 'driving' aids of your voice and whip with the amount you ease the tension on the lunge-rein.

■ *If the horse refuses to stop, work the circles towards the nearest high hedge or wall, then drive him out of the circle and straight into it, at the same time giving the firm command 'halt'.*

■ *Teach the horse not to fall in on the circle by bringing the whip forwards quietly and pointing it at his shoulder.*

■ *If the horse pulls out on the circle, do not pull harder on the lunge rein: rather, lighten the contact and drive him forwards.*

■ *Your horse stops and faces you, then runs*

backwards: run quickly towards him, and he will almost certainly stop. Then lead him back onto the circle.

■ *Your horse stops, turns inwards and changes direction: quickly reverse the aids, bring him to halt with the voice or by driving him into the wall, then start him off again on the correct circle.*

■ *Your horse swings his quarters towards you and heads off out of the circle: drop the whip, bend the knees and lean back against the rein at 45° to his head if possible. For greater control, run the lunge rein through the inside snaffle ring, over the poll and then fasten to the outside ring.*

Long-reining: 1

PROBLEM Many trainers advocate the use of long-reins; but how is long-reining useful, and what exactly does it involve?

SOLUTION Long-reining is a very useful exercise in the training of young horses, as it can teach them the basic rein aids without the added weight and hindrance of the rider. Whereas lungeing involves working on a circle and in one direction at a time, long-reining is more versatile in that the handler can change direction and ask for a bend or flexion each time he turns. Although long-reining must be undertaken carefully, anyone with soft hands and common sense should be able to learn how to drive a horse in long-reins successfully. If the handler is inexperienced, it is wise to practise on an older, experienced horse first, since if both horse and rider are learning there is obviously more scope for misunderstanding and muddles.

The higher the position of the long-reins on the roller – ie the higher the ring through which they are threaded – the greater the potential leverage on the horse's mouth. Certainly this gives great control, but the effect can be sharp and may cause the horse to overbend and to walk with a shortened stride.

Long-reins can be attached in different ways, the various methods originating from different countries; also trainers will adapt these methods to suit their own horses. The British method favours the reins running from the bit (or initially a lunge cavesson), through rings on a lunge roller to the trainer's hands. The handler may stand slightly to one side of the horse so that the outside rein passes around its hindquarters. There are even variations on this method, such as using a saddle instead of a roller, the reins passing through secured stirrup irons on either side. One way is not necessarily right and the other wrong, but different fittings may see different results.

Safety is very important when introducing long-reins. First of all the field or schooling area should be fenced or enclosed in some way so there is no chance of the horse escaping should he be alarmed. The

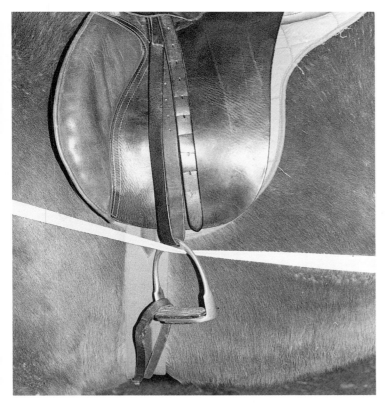

Many people prefer simply to take each rein through the let-down stirrup because they consider this provides a more direct, and so potentially softer feel to the mouth. The stirrups should be secured to the girth to prevent them swinging about.

Introducing horses to traffic whilst long-reining is not a good idea After all, no young horse is predictable, and the handler would have very little control in the event of the horse bolting or shying from his vantage point at the quarters. A rider has more control on board the horse, and is able to use his other natural aids more effectively.

handler should wear a protective riding hat in case the horse kicks out, and also a pair of gloves.

When teaching a youngster for the first time, it is probably advisable to use the rings on a lunge cavesson rather than the bit; as the exercise will be new and possibly alarming, it is not worth running the risk of harming his mouth. Once he has accepted the handler's position at his rear and the feel of the reins on his sides, he should be ready to cope with the feel of the rein contact on his bit.

The trainer must proceed very carefully:
◆ He must allow with the hands, particularly when turning.
◆ The inside hand should ask for flexion, the outside hand must allow the horse's head, neck and shoulder to move freely.
◆ The elbows should be bent but relaxed at all times, never restricting.
◆ Turns in each direction may be carried out, and also transitions through halt and walk. Bending exercises around cones are very useful if the schooling area is large enough; this will involve the handler walking more centrally behind the horse's quarters, and requires a good deal of competence.

Long-reining is a very useful exercise in the training of most young horses, and when combined with lungeing it provides a sound base for the 'building blocks' of schooling.

Long-reining: 2

PROBLEM How do you stop your horse from picking up bad habits on long-reins?

◆ **Raising the head:** If the horse starts to do this, fit the reins on to the bit, then along the horse's sides, passing them through two rings on both sides of a roller, or the secured stirrup irons on a saddle. The handler must not exert a downward action on the reins, but should maintain a good contact. The horse should be kept at a steady walk, the handler keeping his arms relaxed, with a bend in the elbow.

◆ **Dropping the head:** If the horse drops his head and tries to lean on the rein contact, it may be beneficial to fit the reins to the bit, before passing them through the rings on top of the roller. The handler will need to have very soft, light hands, as the reins pass over the horse's back and give a slight lifting action. Heavy hands may cause the horse to come behind the bit and subsequently become stiff and unyielding.

◆ **Overbending to one side:** *The reins may be fitted in this instance using a roller with side rings, or a saddle with secured irons; the inside rein passes directly from the bit to the hand as if it were a lunge line, the other passing through the ring or stirrup iron. This creates an inside bend and encourages the quarters to work, as the outside line passes around the horse's rump.*

◆ **Throwing the head up and down:** *Fitting the reins as for overbending is most suitable for the horse who throws his head about, mainly because there is less chance of the 'backwards' action allowed by other methods. The horse must work forwards into the contact without feeling restricted, which may happen if he throws his head up and down and is pulled in the mouth. If this problem persists it may be a good idea to lunge the horse for a while to help him move forwards and more freely once again.*

Backing

PROBLEM The backing process must always be undertaken carefully and consistently – however, some horses seem to accept this stage of breaking in more happily than others. How can the basics be taught safely and successfully?

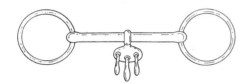

A mouthing bit

Training is usually a two person job, from the safety point of view; youngsters are so unpredictable. While one person is teaching certain tasks, the other can hold the horse and monitor his reactions. Protective safety equipment must be worn by both parties at all times, particularly a riding hat and a pair of gloves.

CAUSE Training young horses is governed, to a certain extent, by trial and error – even the best trainers started somewhere, and learned initially from their own, and other people's mistakes. Anyone with a sound knowledge of effective riding, and who possesses practical experience and patience, is capable of training a youngster. Problems and setbacks usually occur when the trainer's confidence is at a low ebb or his abilities have been questioned: the horse will sense this and will invariably try to dominate the trainer. If he refuses to accept the backing process it is generally because he is aware of his trainer's anxiety, and does not possess the trust or the good manners that should already have been instilled.

SOLUTION It is important that the trainer insists on discipline and manners in all areas of the horse's life – training does not just take place in the schooling area. In his daily life he should be learning respect all the time, and to accept certain rules, such as to walk quietly and to be tied up – though he can still have a good deal of fun.

Tack and equipment should be introduced gradually, stage by stage; in this way the horse should have no reason to be alarmed. Some horses respond most happily to a key bit: a jointed snaffle with mouthing keys at the centre. These bits may be old-fashioned, but they fulfil a useful purpose in allowing the horse to become accustomed just to the feel of the bit in his mouth, before rein or rider is introduced. Later evasions with the rein contact may be prevented if the horse is comfortable just with the feel of a bit, before he is expected to understand about contact. He may be left in the stable for short periods wearing a bridle and key bit, though under supervision in case he should panic.

Most horses will not make a fuss about accepting weight on their back if it is introduced gradually in the stable, starting with a lightweight rug and a loose surcingle, and progressing to a roller over a piece of sponge. Again the horse should trust the handler, and should have no reason to suspect the roller will hurt as long as his experience of rugs and surcingles has been happy and stress free. At the next stage he may be led outside the stable with a roller on his back, so that he gets used to the feeling of tightness and friction around his belly as his legs move; providing it is not too tight and is done up gradually, he should take it in his stride.

The saddle should also be introduced in the stable, an assistant holding the horse as it is placed gently on his back. The girth should be done up gradually, and the horse allowed to eat a haynet or to move around the stable (though he should be supervised all the time for this stage of breaking in). There is no reason for him to become in any way frightened at this stage, unless he was not previously accustomed to the roller. One step at a time is the rule here, and it is one worth remembering at all times.

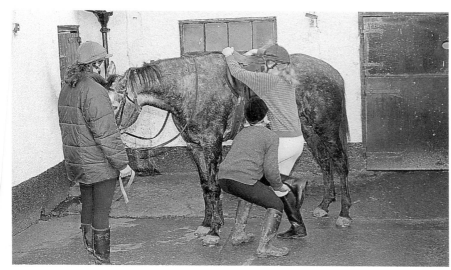

Introducing the horse to the feel of having a rider on his back.

Note that there is an assistant present to hold the horse's head and reassure him with a calming word.

The helper gives the rider a leg up to lean her weight across the saddle. Every movement is made slowly and in a relaxed manner (see also page 28).

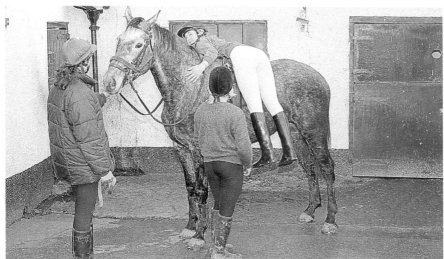

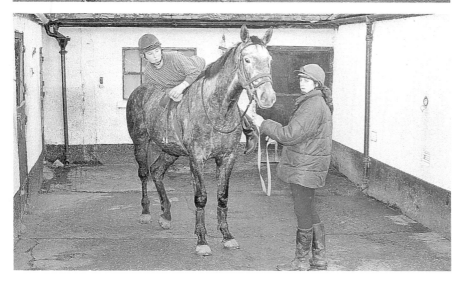

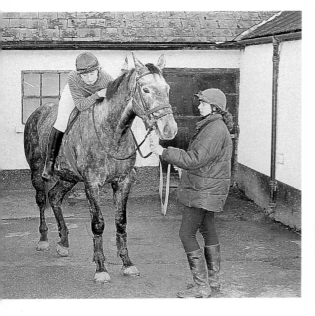

Having got the horse used to the feel of a rider leaning over his back, the next stage is to sit astride. Note how the rider keeps a low position which not only makes it less alarming for the horse but which makes it easier to slip off his back should trouble occur.

Once he seems happy with this arrangement it is time for the assistant to lead him forward and then for horse and rider to go solo! The confines of this small yard are ideal as any difficult situation can be easily contained.

Leaning over the horse's back in a confined area or school may be useful, though this must be attempted carefully. If the horse is used to being groomed then he will not mind the trainer putting an arm over his back, and he should not object to the next stage when the trainer partially leans across his back. Once he is accustomed to this, the trainer can very gradually and gently take the weight off his feet, so that eventually all his weight is over the horse's back. An assistant handler should be holding the horse's head, watching his reaction and talking softly to him, and the trainer should stroke the horse and pat him encouragingly. Both trainer and assistant should be wearing protective safety wear.

There will always be criticism of certain training methods, and indeed there is some risk in leaning over the horse while he is in the stable. However, it must be stressed that trainers should take things slowly and develop their own methods: if they consider a horse is sensible enough to accept a certain exercise or procedure, then so be it; as with everything, they can only learn from their mistakes. Providing safety is a constant consideration and progress is not rushed in any way, there is no reason why a young horse should not accept the backing process. There are countless books on the subject, and many professionals available to help if required. Trainers must just develop an understanding with each horse, and have confidence in their own abilities.

CAUSE   The problem horse may raise its head when the handler attempts to place the bit in its mouth; this may be accompanied by pacing backwards, or pulling back if the horse is restrained. Even the smallest pony can place its head in an awkward position, and in the case of a large horse the head can quickly be out of reach.

SOLUTION   The handler must not get angry and frustrated, and should not physically chastise the horse, as this will encourage it to become headshy. The handler should be firm but gentle, making sure he is not banging the horse's teeth or hurting its mouth with the bit. The horse should not feel restricted, so it is best to have an assistant hold a headcollar and leadrope attached around its neck, or to bridle it within the stable.

The handler should hold the bridle in his right hand about halfway down its length, then put his right hand under the horse's neck and around the front of its face, so that its head is cradled by his arm. With the left hand the handler may place the bit (perhaps coated with honey or sugar) in the horse's mouth. If the horse clamps its teeth shut, he might gently place a finger in the corner of its mouth, as the ticklish sensation encourages the horse to open wide. At this point the bit is inserted carefully and the headpiece placed over the ears, taking care not to pull or pinch them. If the horse is generally wary of its ears being touched, handlers should make a point of touching and grooming them daily, so the horse becomes accustomed to this and does not anticipate discomfort.

SOLUTION   Handlers should make sure the bit is fitted correctly and hangs comfortably, and may find changing the style of bit helps. For instance, a rollered mouthpiece gives a little more play within the mouth, whilst a ported mouthpiece may prevent the horse putting his tongue over the bit. However, any change of bit must be considered carefully; it may be that the rider needs instead to change his style of riding and maintain a firmer contact; or perhaps the horse is bored and needs more stimulation to divert his attention?

Difficult to bridle

PROBLEM   Some horses also develop the problem of being 'bridle shy'; they are generally wary or disobedient when bridled, resisting the handler's attempts at tacking up, and even showing fear. How can this be overcome?

Tongue over the bit

PROBLEM   Some horses develop the habit of placing their tongue over the bit, either when being exercised or just standing still. How can this be cured?

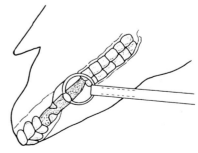

(above) Check that the bit rests on the toothless part of the jawbones (the bars)

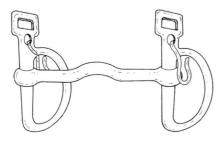

(left) A port-mouthed, sliding cheek Kimblewick

Chewing the bit

PROBLEM When the horse chews or rattles his bit, it becomes in effect an evasion. What causes the problem in the first place, and how can it be prevented in the future?

CAUSE Chewing the bit can be one of the most annoying evasions from the rider's point of view, due to the loud rattling noise and accompanying head movement. The degree of the problem can vary from a slight movement of the horse's teeth, to exaggerated head-shaking. The end result is non-acceptance of the contact, and therefore potentially a vice should the habit become established. Essentially the horse is not relaxed, particularly in his jaw, and this in turn means the head and therefore the neck are tense, which will inevitably affect the 'looseness' of the horse's whole body. He will not be working in a correct outline, and will almost certainly be behind the bit. There are several circumstances which may cause this habit:

◆ It may originate from the backing stage, when the bit and bridle were first introduced. Key bits can prove very useful, but if they are left on for long periods over several weeks, they may encourage too much playing within the mouth.

◆ A bit that hangs too low in the mouth will also encourage chewing, even if it was fitted correctly before the horse was schooled – once he picks up a certain habit it may prove difficult to break.

Take care when fitting a flash or a grakle: the top strap should lie immediately below the prominent cheek bone otherwise it will rub; however, it should not be any lower or it may impede the horse's breathing, and anyway it is not effective if it is too low. Note that a grakle noseband is not permitted in pure dressage competitions.

◆ The problem may only emerge when the horse is tense or excited, or wants to get somewhere quickly – perhaps at an event or before a race. In this case the first priority is to alleviate the tension and nerves, particularly if the event which causes the excitement is a regular occurrence.

◆ There may be an existing physical problem, such as ill-fitting tack or perhaps a sore mouth caused by sharp teeth or sores. Anything that causes discomfort around the head could provoke the horse into evading the contact and creating a diversion.

SOLUTION So what can you do about this problem?

◆ Using a fixed, rather than a jointed bit mouthpiece may improve the situation as it will not move around so much within the mouth, encouraging the horse to relax his jaw and accept the contact.

◆ A flash or a grakle noseband may prevent excessive jaw movement, providing that it is correctly fitted and is not too tight. There is a fine line when using such nosebands: acceptably tight and the horse will be encouraged to be submissive; restricted too severely, and he may spend the whole time fighting it.

◆ Incorrect riding may be the cause, for instance if the rider is heavy-handed or does not provide enough impulsion so the horse falls behind the bit. He must be driven forwards into a light contact, and made to use his hindquarters with his hocks well underneath him. And the rider must be ready to allow with the hand, so the horse is not afraid to accept the contact: as soon as he relaxes the jaw and accepts the bit, the rider should give with the rein so the horse is 'rewarded' for relaxing. Once he begins to respond as required, careful schooling is needed, in the same manner as if the horse were behind the bit (see page 56). As long as a light, still contact is maintained, the bit-chewing problem should become less, and in time the horse's outline will improve.

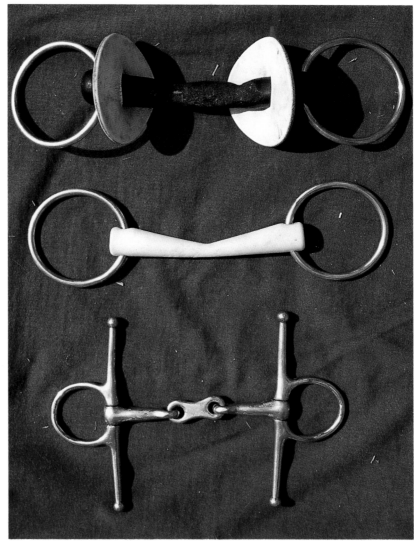

Three useful bits: at top, a well chewed loose-ring, slightly mullen-mouth rubber snaffle; the rubber ring-guards prevent any possibility of pinching so the whole arrangement is soft and comfortable. At centre: a Nathe loose-ring snaffle with a shaped mouthpiece; horses do seem to like these. At bottom: a French link snaffle with long cheek pieces; the latter should help with steering and to keep the horse straight, although the link snaffle can make some fussy horses that chew and fiddle even worse.

Saddling problems

PROBLEM Some young horses are unco-operative when their handler tries to place a saddle on their backs, flinching or moving away. What are the causes of this reaction, and how can the problem be remedied?

A saddle-raising pad; these and 'jelly pads' are particularly useful when saddling young horses which inevitably change shape in the course of their training and are therefore more prone to rubs and sores.

SOLUTION Many young horses are wary of strange new occurrences in their lives, and fitting unaccustomed tack is no exception. Thus it may take them some time to get used to the strange weight of the saddle placed on their back – though providing the backing process is taken slowly there should be no reason for any horse to be alarmed. And if a horse is initially frightened, then the process is being rushed and the trainer should continue to use a roller or surcingle until he is more relaxed about the situation. It is to be expected that some horses will be apprehensive and wary; in such a case the trainer should place the saddle quietly on the horse's back and just allow him time to get used to it.

Problems tend to arise when the saddle is banged down on a horse's back by a careless handler, and may be exacerbated if the horse is quite large. In this situation the trainer should stand on a solid box so the saddle may be lowered, rather than lifted onto the back. Unless he takes this sort of precaution, this problem may become worse later on, because each time the horse is tacked up he may be anticipating discomfort and this will tend to have an accumulative effect – until one day he retaliates.

In those cases where a considerate saddling procedure has always been adhered to, it may be that the horse is suffering from cold back syndrome, when the muscles tense up, particularly in cold weather. This is similar to the human who hunches his shoulders against the cold winter wind, and finds at the end of the day that they are sore. The next day he will hunch them even more, since when sore, they are more sensitive to the cold. Thus the horse with a cold back has hunched-up quarters which are tender when subjected to weight. He will dip his back when the saddle is placed on it, and may well dip down again, or even more, when the rider mounts. This situation can be eased if the horse's quarters are kept warm with a rug or blanket at all times, and if he is massaged before being tacked up. The affected area should be rubbed with firm circular movements, and using liquid liniment or muscle relaxant is especially effective.

An ill-fitting saddle may be the cause of the trouble: it will be causing discomfort when the horse is ridden, which of course he associates with the saddle being fitted. This is a common problem with youngsters because they change shape as their training progresses so their original saddle ends up not fitting in all the right places. For this reason it may be sensible to begin training with a synthetic or secondhand leather saddle; it will be much cheaper in the long run. A horse's saddle should always be fitted by a member of the Master Saddlers' Association, and checked regularly for damage or pressure points. Uncomfortable numnahs and saddle covers may cause a similar problem, and should always lie flush to the skin.

A back problem such as muscle or ligament damage will also cause discomfort, as will a heavy or unbalanced rider.

Although all of these problems certainly do cause pain when the horse is ridden, he may in fact be suffering from 'fear by association',

a) A general purpose saddle, with riser and 'sheepskin' num-nah, often used when the saddle lies too 'flat' on the horse's back. Keep a close eye on this sort of numnah when the horse is moulting, because the hair tends to work into a hard ball at the pressure points under the cantle and can make the horse very sore.

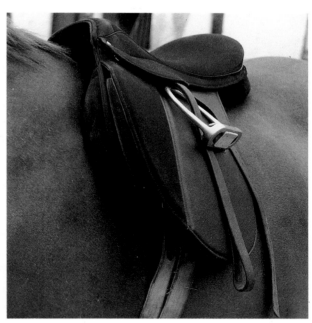

b) A fabric saddle; this style is becoming increasingly popular. They are generally lighter than a leather saddle, but need frequent brushing if they are to stay looking smart.

c) A forward-cut jumping saddle; this appears to be quite high over the wither, which would effectively position the rider's weight too far back on the horse's back; however, with the rider in the jumping position this effect would be nullified.

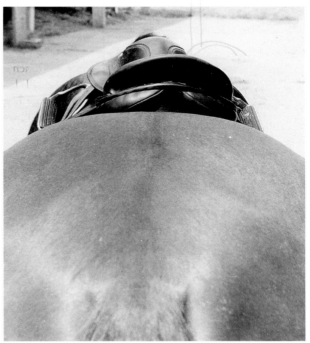

d) Plenty of room for the horse's backbone, but it would be better if the saddle were square on the horse's back!

knowing that when the saddle is placed on his back there is pain to follow. A veterinary surgeon or back specialist should examine him, and the rider should be assessed to determine whether he is moving with the horse's rhythm, or banging on its back.

Whatever causes the horse's back to dip or flinch, it is always a good idea to keep it warm; this includes using an exercise sheet in cold weather. Also the rider should use a mounting block at all times, and always maintain a deep seat with good rhythm and balance. And finally the saddle should be checked regularly, and always placed on the horse's back with care.

Dashing off when mounted

PROBLEM Some horses try to race off the minute the rider lands in the saddle. Why is this, and how can it be overcome?

SOLUTION Tacking up may not be a problem, but sometimes a horse fidgets or dashes off when mounted. This is an indication that the backing process has been rushed a little, or that the horse anticipates pain through the rider banging down on his back or jabbing him in the mouth. The horse should be accustomed to the rider leaning over his back and accepting the saddle – if he is naturally nervous or high-spirited it may prove useful to lunge him first to remove his excess energy.

On arrival at the mounting area or school he should be walked around a little to allow any initial excitement to subside. An assistant should then halt the horse next to a mounting block, holding each side of the bit but making sure that he is not directly in front of the horse. The rider must mount quickly; if he is not very nimble he should practise on another horse so that there is no awkward hopping about. He must also land quietly in the saddle, even taking his weight forwards a little. The assistant should tell the horse to stand, and may carry a whip to tap the horse's shoulder if he walks forwards. A verbal 'Stand' will also help. It is important not to dawdle about, so tighten the girth quickly. The stirrup leathers should be adjusted already, so that the horse does not have time to get bored and fidgety.

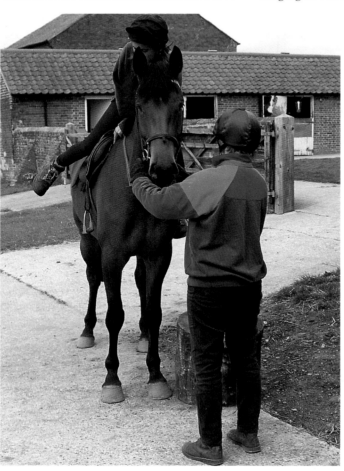

It is essential that the mounting procedure is organised, quick and slick: a mounting block should always be used, the stirrups should be already adjusted to the correct length for the rider, and the assistant should know exactly where to stand; and how to hold the horse – held too tight or too strongly and he may really start to panic.

Misbehaving when being saddled

This calls for assistance, and such behaviour must be stopped as soon as possible! Once any possible physical cause has been eliminated, the handler must be very firm and authoritative. The backing process must be taken back to basics if necessary, using a roller or surcingle until the horse accepts each step with confidence. When it comes to putting on the saddle, he should be held firmly at the head, rather than tied up which may prove dangerous.

As soon as the horse attempts to fidget or lie down, he must be encouraged to stand still, using a whip if necessary, and a stern 'No!' in a loud, firm voice. If he runs backwards it may be useful to have two assistants hold a lunge line placed around his rump, so that he feels as if he is backing into something and moves forwards.

PROBLEM A high-spirited or disobedient horse may react strongly to being tacked up: for instance, an unco-operative youngster may lie down or even throw himself around as the saddle is fitted or the girth tightened. What should you do?

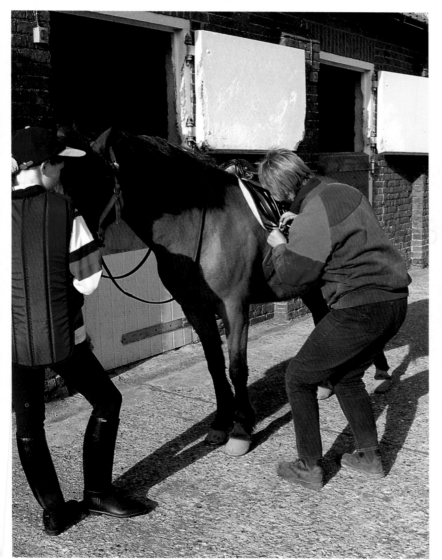

A girth with elastic inserts (above) makes a tremendous difference with a horse that is particularly ticklish or difficult to girth up. Even so, take the usual precaution of having an assistant to stand in front of the horse whilst you tighten his girth. Some ponies seem to feel threatened by you towering over them, so try to keep your head below their eyeline when girthing up (left)

Sensitive to the leg

PROBLEM Some youngsters seem extra-sensitive to the leg, and this may cause them to run away from, rather than to accept, the leg aids. How can a trainer teach a horse to respond sensibly to the aids?

CAUSE To a certain extent this problem is indeed about sensitivity, some horses being more ticklish than others and extra-responsive. However, the essence of the problem is insufficient schooling, because even the most sensitive horses, if well trained, will accept and respond to the leg. The problem horse may run forwards when the leg aids are applied, perhaps lifting his head and losing his rhythm, and if he is already heavy on the forehand he may be even more inclined to run through the rider's hands – this indicates a fundamental lack of balance, again probably the result of insufficient training.

Basically as far as the horse is concerned, the leg aids just mean 'go faster', and a pull on the reins means 'slow down', instead of leg and hand being used in conjunction with one another, a fact which must be instilled into both horse and rider from an early age.

SOLUTION So, how should we overcome this problem?
◆ The long-term solution is to school the horse carefully, using plenty of transitions, initially on the lunge or long-reins and without the rider.
◆ Once the horse has good rhythm and balance, upward and downward transitions will help his balance, the rider using a firm leg but slightly blocking with the hand; the horse needs to learn not to rush forwards as soon as the leg aid is applied.
◆ Half-halting will help to get the message across, when the horse's forward movement is checked with the rein whilst the leg maintains the impulsion; this results in improved submission to the aids, and better engagement and control. Repeating the process should in time see marked improvement, as long as the rider learns to give with the hand as the horse relaxes and does what he is asked.
◆ The owner can make sure tender spots are not irritated, by avoiding grooming with a dandy brush around the horse's sides, or using a girth that pinches.
◆ The rider's leg position may be too far back, aggravating the horse and causing him to rush forwards. Leg aids should be as gentle as possible, squeezing rather than kicking and of course not using spurs.
◆ Should none of the above suggestions bring a positive result, it may be necessary to use a slightly stronger bit, at least until the horse has improved. A mild snaffle is the ideal bit in which to school a youngster, but there is little point in battling against a horse's pull if he is determined not to listen to the rider's half-halt aids. If the desired result can be achieved using a bit with a slightly stronger action, the rider can always return to the original bit once the horse has learnt the correct response.

This rider's lower leg is too far back; this alone may cause the horse to rush forwards. The rider's whole position should be checked by a knowledgeable instructor, because some other fault of position may be causing the lower leg to slip back: the rider's body may be tipping forwards too much, the stirrups may be too short, he or she may be losing balance and resting on the horse's neck.

Schooling could well start with that most basic of schooling movements a) the half-halt (above); this should improve the horse's submissiveness, as will b) leg-yielding (below), which teaches him to move his quarters away from the leg whilst remaining soft and in balance.

As he improves, lateral work such as c) shoulder-in (top) and d) half-pass (above) will help to lighten his forehand even more, thereby minimising any inclination to rush off. This horse's shoulder-in (c) in particular demonstrates a light, or raised forehand.

Avoid overfacing the youngster

PROBLEM It is quite easy to overface the willing youngster which is learning quickly. How can trainers be sure of educating their horses without overfacing them?

SOLUTION Unfortunately there are no hard and fast rules concerning the training of horses. Yes, there are guidelines, but these may vary from one horse to another, as all are individuals. Overfacing is caused by a combination of two things: lack of maturity or confidence on the horse's part, and overzealousness or inexperience on the trainer's.

A big mistake is to start the horse's training too early, and it is really not a good idea to attempt to back him until he is three. The two-year-old will not be either physically or emotionally ready to cope with such training – besides which he should be enjoying what is in essence his childhood. So, basic training can be started when the horse is three; he should then be allowed a break over the winter, before his training is resumed in his fourth year. As previously stated, there are no hard and fast rules, but following these guidelines is considered by the majority of trainers to bring the best results.

Before he begins, the trainer must identify exactly what he is aiming for in his initial training programme: for example a rounded topline, an improved engagement of the hocks, and a good sense of balance and rhythm. The horse's paces and outline will, of course, improve with maturity, as will muscle development and general form.

Having established what he is aiming for, the trainer must then evaluate the horse: for

A young horse needs plenty of time to grow and develop, and serious training should never be attempted until he is at least three years old: physically his frame will be unable to cope with hard work and he will risk strain or injury; psychologically he will almost certainly find such pressure too stressful and as a result may become tense, resentful, excitable, nervous or bolshy – traits which normally he might not show at all.

instance is he willing, or highly strung, or immature? His outlook is bound to affect the schooling programme, as some animals will need more time and patience than others according to their temperament and natural ability. It may be useful for trainers to set rough goals for themselves, aiming, say, in the initial six months for the horse to have accepted with happy submission the weight and authority of a rider, and the rider to have assumed control and respect. Specific goals regarding school movements and paces should be avoided, however, as it is this which may lead to overfacing a horse; besides, there is little point in rushing the initial stages. Providing the horse is of a calm nature and can maintain forward movement with reasonable balance, he can be expected to learn and progress later on, with careful schooling.

It is always best to finish a training session on a good note, and in this the trainer should trust his own judgement and sometimes play a situation 'by ear'. For instance, if the horse has successfully completed a task before the end of the lesson, it may be just as productive to finish the session early and reward him with a treat, than to move on to something else or repeat the process endlessly and risk confusing or boring him so that he loses enthusiasm.

Breaking bonds

SOLUTION   This situation usually stems from anxiety or excitement caused by a lack of company, when the horse is normally kept all on his own; or because he has forged too great an attachment to a certain animal during his free time (this particular problem is discussed in more depth on page 41). Perhaps the horse is stabled away from other animals, and is anxious because he can hear, but not see them. All horses thrive on companionship, particularly youngsters, and instinctively want to bond with other horses; just the reassurance of another horse in the same field will help develop a horse's confidence, and even a donkey or a goat is better than nothing! The horse is a herd animal and so his need for companionship is always paramount: so if the only time he sees other animals is when he is schooled, then it is quite understandable that he will not want to concentrate!

One option is to move the horses adjacent to the schooling area to another field for a while, although this may not be practical. In any case, the horse will need to become accustomed to working in company, for when he goes to a show or an event. So, how to proceed if the other horses are still nearby and proving to be a distraction?

When entering the school, the rider should make every attempt to calm the horse down, walking on a loose rein and using a soothing voice. The horse should be walked around the outside track of the school, so he is not avoiding working near the other horses, but is learning to ignore them. The rider should concentrate on schooling the horse as he normally would, using a varied programme of transitions and school movements, beginning in walk to loosen up the muscles gradually. Whilst going past the other horses, he should use a firm leg, perhaps turning the horse's head away slightly so that concentration is not lost. If the horse does not settle, he may then be worked in a corner away from the others, gradually being ridden closer.

A fitted fly fringe with ears may help the horse to concentrate, as outside noises are then reduced considerably. As a last resort blinkers might be tried, although this can never be a long-term solution, as the horse may come to rely on them, getting used to limited vision – so when they are taken off, he is even worse.

A much better policy is to take the horse away for riding lessons, and to shows and events, even if only to walk around and take in the atmosphere. Every opportunity should be taken so he can mix and associate with others, whether it be for a hack or a schooling session. And once he is used to spending time in company, he will undoubtedly settle and relax when in the vicinity of other animals.

PROBLEM   Some horses are unwilling to work properly when in the vicinity of other horses, particularly if they are friends or stable-mates. What can the rider do to alleviate this problem?

As long as the horse is busy and occupied he will be less likely to spend time fretting for a companion. So take him to events and shows, even if you don't intend to compete; the more opportunity he has to learn to work and settle down in exciting surroundings, the quicker he will learn to concentrate when you tell him to.

Overcoming nervousness

PROBLEM Young horses are easily scared, spooking at anything and sometimes making themselves even more nervous. How can riders give their horses more confidence?

SOLUTION All young horses have the potential to be nervous and scared, although the way in which they are brought up will affect their temperament to a certain extent. The naturally highly strung horse may always be unpredictable, but owners can prevent excess nerves by careful training. From the moment the horse is brought home his training should start, if only to establish an understanding relationship and mutual respect. Once the horse has confidence in his owner he will be much more relaxed altogether, and therefore less likely to shy at things.

Sensible handling is very important: the horse whose owner is always shouting and waving his hands about, or dropping things around the yard will be constantly on edge – or those who leave plastic bags blowing around, or a broom in the stable to be knocked down will make the horse thoroughly jumpy and just waiting for the next disruption. The owner must instil confidence in his horse by gentle but firm handling, talking to him all the time and never making sudden movements. Remember, too, that horses can sense fear or anxiety in their handler and will react accordingly. Of course there is no point in shielding the horse from everyday occurrences so as not to upset him – traffic, tractors, gates banging and so on, are all part of the horse's education, and knowing about them will help his confidence when he hacks out later on.

Owners should be aiming for an all-round education for their horses, coupled with common sense and patience. This is all very well if an owner has looked after a horse since he was a foal, but what if he has learned bad habits from other people? If the horse is fairly young he may still be able to learn to settle down and gain confidence; but with an older horse it may be more difficult because his nerves may have established themselves.

When schooling, a rider should always ride through any problems, offering encouragement all the time. For instance, if the horse will not go past a certain corner of the school, he should take the horse away and trot him on a circle at some distance from the area, but he should get closer each time he circles, approaching it gradually and riding past authoritatively. Even if initially the horse has to be led beyond it, he must go past that spot so he has at least learned to put *some* trust in his rider.

It may be useful to accustom the horse to certain scary situations with some help from an assistant: for instance, rustling a plastic bag or leading the horse over brightly coloured poles.

Owners may also wish to turn the horse out in a field within earshot of a road, or near to working farm equipment. The daily noise and bustle will acclimatise him to traffic noises, so that he is more relaxed and confident when he is taken on the roads. The more he can learn while he is still young, the more 'rounded' his character will be later on in life.

Use shoulder-in to negotiate a horse past something he finds spooky or frightening: if you turn his head towards it he will swing his quarters right out into the road, besides which you risk him shying violently; if you use shoulder-in so that his head is turned away from the object, it is easier to keep him under control, and 'between hand and leg'.

Independence

SOLUTION It is important that horses develop their own sense of independence, and allowing a horse to become too attached to a companion is inadvisable: throughout its life there will be times when they will have to be apart, and reliance on another animal will always prove upsetting in the long run. Most horses move establishments several times over the years, making new friends and learning new routines, and many seem to forget that their old friends even existed as soon as they arrive – but others pine and will display very real signs of being ill.

A policy which generally works is to balance the horse's relationships when he is young, so he has his own space for eating and sleeping at night, with enough peace and quiet to settle down, but companionship during the day. He may be turned out with other horses, providing the field or paddock is big enough – about one acre for each horse is the accepted way to assess this. When stabled, it is important that the horses can see and hear each other, but not be so close that they are cramped – the pony stabling at certain riding establishments is grossly inadequate, where groups of ponies are kept in small barns or looseboxes. Once a horse shows he is unwilling to leave a mate, it is important to act soon. The two must be separated for a period of time each day, no matter how much protesting occurs. Certainly youngsters, however, have short memories and will soon get over their apparent anguish when presented with a bowl of food. The time that the two animals spend apart should be lengthened gradually until they are used to being on their own for longer periods. Again, food is a useful ploy: a haynet to keep them occupied and a few succulent treats will go a long way to easing the trauma.

When a horse is taken away to be schooled it is important that he recognises the difference between work and play. When turned out with his friend, he will obviously romp around and get rid of excess energy in the field – but it is essential that he learns that schooling is most definitely work, and that he must then forget playing around and listen to his rider.

Providing the separation process is done gradually and handled very carefully, there is no reason for any long-term anxiety.

Once horses are older, keeping two close companions apart will be like trying to separate a loving elderly couple, and one may not be prepared to do anything at all without the other. Like this, the companion may have to be taken along to shows and events too, in order to 'keep the peace', or be turned out next to the schooling area. Obviously this is not a desirable scenario at all and very impractical – so action to resolve the problem at an early age is essential.

PROBLEM All horses need companionship, particularly when young and mischievous, but too close a bond between two animals can spell trouble, and may lead to an extreme reluctance to be separated. How can independence be achieved without too much disruption?

Fencing must be obviously stout and robust when separating horses; if they can see it is solid, they will be less likely to try to climb over or through it in their anxiety to get back to their companion. If it is in the least weak or suspect, they will keep trying to get out.

Stiffness

PROBLEM During training, many youngsters develop stiffness. What can riders do to overcome this setback, and how might they help the horse to become more supple?

CAUSE It is quite usual for a youngster to show signs of stiffness, particularly at the beginning of his training when his body is still suppling up and changing shape. The problem generally lies along the horse's back, or in some cases in the neck. This may be caused by a physical problem, originally caused by the horse rolling violently or falling over, perhaps resulting in a damaged or bruised muscle; nowadays there are many back specialists and veterinary surgeons who deal with such problems every day, as the subject has gained much recognition over the years. If riders suspect an underlying problem, then a simple examination by a professional will determine this.

Check the saddle: a badly fitting saddle may be causing discomfort, particularly if the horse has changed shape since it was first fitted. Synthetic saddles are often useful for youngsters, as they are reasonably cheap to buy and are light in weight. However, they do sometimes change shape when stressed or stretched, and even if this is slight, the weight-bearing surface along the horse's back may be altered. A basic, second-hand general purpose saddle is probably the best investment for the youngster, unless of course owners can afford to invest in a brand-new saddle which may be changed when the horse is fully developed. The numnah or saddle cloth must be smooth and comfortable, and of course the girth should not be pinching or causing discomfort. However, ill-fitting tack is not usually the reason for stiffness, and generally it is simply that most youngsters are just not yet supple enough, something that will improve with careful schooling.

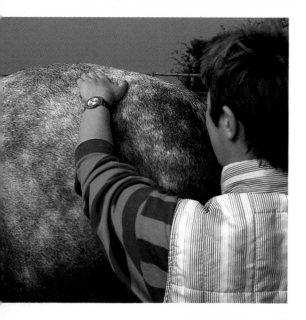

Always have a back specialist check your horse if you suspect a problem; also heat lamps can be bought or hired for use at home, and are most effective for relieving stiff or strained muscles.

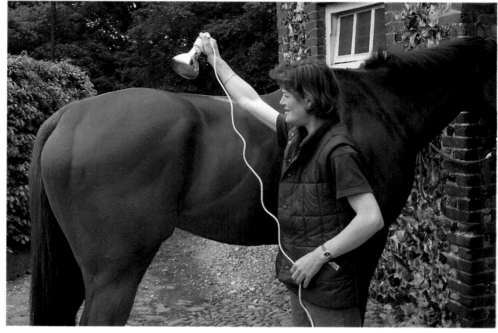

SOLUTION

So, what may be done to help the horse become more supple?

- The horse's body should always be sufficiently warmed up before beginning a schooling session. The walk is the best pace with which to commence the warm-up, as it uses more muscles at any one time than other gaits. Walk with a long rein, and allow the horse to stretch his neck, and use basic school movements and frequent transitions; this will give a good basis for further work. Some trot work may then be introduced, the rider gradually taking up the contact and working the horse in.

- Riders must be careful to use their own weight cautiously, and not bump about on the horse's back or do a great deal of sitting trot. It is quite acceptable to stand in the stirrups and lift the weight from off the horse's back during canter work and ground pole work, so that he can really use his back without the hindrance of the rider's weight bumping about in the saddle. General suppling exercises will reduce stiffness eventually, such as transitions, decreasing and increasing circles, school movements and bending. The horse must at all times be encouraged to engage the hocks more effectively, by using firm, correct leg aids and light hands.

- Lungeing will help to minimise stiffness, both with and without the rider.

- Ground pole work will also help: poles may be set up a horse's canter stride apart, so they can be used for walk, trot and canter. Riders can estimate this by using three of their own strides, then they should ride over the poles to find out if the distance is correct. Three walk strides should fit comfortably between the poles, and an assistant can move them until the precise distance has been found (it is a good idea to take a note of this measurement so that it can be used again for the individual horse; this is always especially helpful when schooling alone). Two trot strides and one canter stride will also fit in between the poles, and these can be raised at one or both ends to encourage further suppling of the back. The horse should be allowed to stretch down through the neck as he goes over the poles, with the rider in a slightly forward position so as to take his weight off the horse's back.

Allow the horse to stretch and relax as he works over the poles; his back should swing rhythmically, allowing easier flexion in his joints and thereby helping his whole body to become more supple. This pony could show a rounder, longer topline with a lower head and neck in order for the exercise to be of optimum benefit.

Rearing

PROBLEM
Rearing is one of the most extreme actions a young horse can take to dislodge its rider. What are the causes behind this problem, and what can be done to resolve it?

Make sure your weight is well forwards if the horse manages a full rear, and try to throw your arms around his neck. Your head is the heaviest part of your body, so make a particular effort to keep it down to one side of the horse's neck; like this it is easier to slip off altogether if you have to.

CAUSE
In most cases, rearing can be regarded as total defiance and must never be treated lightly; the horse is evading all contact with the bit and refusing to go forwards. However, although in most cases the horse is being plain disobedient, it may be the rider's fault that he is behaving in this way. If he is not given enough natural exercise and freedom to kick around when young, his exuberance and pent-up energy may surface when he is under saddle. Therefore it is essential that the young horse is turned out every day for as long as possible, so he has time to expend his high spirits in the field.

Another cause of rearing could be excessive feeding. Owners must work out their horse's diet according to his individual needs, taking into account his age, his temperament, and the amount of work he is doing. If too many high-energy feeds are being given without sufficient exercise to burn off all the energy produced, the horse will call upon any natural instincts he can think of to use it up.

Badly fitting tack may also be just cause for rearing, so all equipment must be correctly and professionally fitted. One of the most common tack-related problems is an ill-fitting bit. If it has sharp edges or is hurting any part of the horse's mouth when he moves forward, the most obvious way that he would try to evade the pain is to go upwards or backwards, away from it. Likewise a bit that is too strong, or a heavy-handed rider, will provoke even the most obedient and docile horse into showing his discomfort.

SOLUTION
It is quite possible that the horse is scared, and in this instance he may also try to spin round, or to run from whatever he is afraid of – this could be anything from a rustling paper bag to a particularly pungent smell. This situation must be treated with great circumspection, as the horse may just be trying his rider out, or he may be being silly, in which case firm riding and an authoritative tone may be all that is needed. However, if he is genuinely frightened, a battle between horse and rider may leave him fearful of this particular thing for life. First of all it may be best to avoid the problem until he has calmed down. Then a helping hand to lead him past the offending object often helps, although the assistant must stay at arms' length in case the horse rears and he is caught with the forelegs.

It is not possible for a horse to rear properly when he has forward movement, unless the rear is part of a plunge or a spin in the opposite direction. Riders should therefore always be sure to ride forwards with plenty of impulsion and firm leg aids; the hands should be still, with a quiet contact. Generally the horse will give warning signs of a potential rear: one of these is jibbing, when he refuses to go forwards and fidgets, perhaps putting in half-rears and bounces – at this point it is imperative that he is driven forwards. The horse also needs to be equally balanced on both hind legs to rear effectively, so when he jibs, or the rider feels his front legs leaving the ground, he could try bending the neck to one side and applying a strong inside leg. The horse's hindlegs will not be carrying equal weight when he is bent sharply one way or another – and if the rider can turn the horse onto a small circle, keeping his hands very low and the horse's neck bent, so much the better.

If this fails and the horse manages a full rear, the rider must act fast. If he is taken unawares, grabbing some mane or holding onto the horse's neck may help. To lose balance and hang onto the reins could be dangerous, as the horse could be pulled over backwards, damaging both parties. If a rider feels the horse overbalancing, he should take his feet out of the stirrups and get out of the way as quickly as possible.

One method of preventing a full rear has been implemented successfully by the American trainer, Monty Roberts. When the horse gathers himself to rear or even lifts his feet off the floor, the rider should lean forwards and tap the horse on his girth area with a whip. This should shock him into coming down. The rider must sit up again quickly and drive the horse forwards, to prevent him having another go at standing up.

Bucking

CAUSE Bucking is something all horses do, whether it is a quick caper when they are turned out, or a rodeo session in the school. Because young horses are still learning, a certain amount of exuberance is acceptable, and not cause for chastisement. So, what might cause a horse to buck?

PROBLEM All young horses need to play, and most work off their excess energy in the field. But what can be done about the horse which constantly bucks under saddle?

- ◆ The most genuine reason for consistent bucking under saddle is pain or discomfort: the horse may be finding it hard to get used to the unaccustomed feel of the saddle, and perhaps the situation is exacerbated by a crumpled numnah or tight girth. Care should be taken that the saddle itself is correctly fitted, bearing in mind that the young horse will change shape as his muscles develop, and all other equipment – bit, bridle and boots – should also be comfortable and well fitting.

- ◆ The rider could be at fault, tugging at the reins or bouncing on top of the horse's back. Exercises without stirrups will improve his balance and deepen his seat, and lunge lessons will prove beneficial.

- ◆ Assuming the rider is of the correct weight and height for the horse, a genuine back problem could be the cause. It could be a temporary ailment caused by rolling in a confined space, or it could be a more long-term problem.

- ◆ Pain anywhere in the horse's body could cause bucking. For instance, discomfort in the hindquarters or hocks will make it difficult for the horse to carry weight, and his natural reaction will be to want to remove the rider. Examination by a veterinary surgeon or back specialist (such as an osteopath or chiropractor) will confirm whether or not the horse has a physical problem, and riders can help to prevent further discomfort by using a mounting block and always warming up the horse's muscles before schooling.

This young horse is obviously enjoying a good lark-about! His rider's position is good, however, and she is not perturbed in the least by his antics – the position of her lower leg is slightly more forward, and with the weight in the heel, thus helping to keep her firmly in the saddle.

In the second photograph things are now taking a more serious turn, but the rider is coping admirably, her weight still firmly in the lower leg and heel, the body straight up rather than forwards, and the head up. Enough is enough, and in a minute she will drive the horse forwards with heels, voice and stick if necessary.

If none of the above reasons are causing the horse to buck, one may assume that he is being simply disobedient and naughty; an occasional buck may be allowed, but consistent bucking is dangerous. So, how can the rider stop a horse bucking?

SOLUTION ◆ The horse will find it easier to buck with his head low down or between his legs. If the rider feels him doing this, he should drive him forwards and try to lift the head. He should take his weight in the stirrups, as sitting deep in the saddle may result in a painful jolt through his back.

◆ Once the horse begins to buck, the rider is in danger of becoming a passenger with no control of direction or pace; he should give short checks on alternate reins, so the horse is not able to lean on a consistent contact to balance himself.

◆ A loud reprimand is a must – young horses should learn to recognise and respond to a sharp 'No'.

◆ Providing the rider stays in the centre of balance, he should be able to stay on board and drive the horse forwards. It is quite acceptable for him to hold on to a piece of mane to help him keep his balance, or to bridge the reins across the neck for extra security.

The next concern is, how might bucking be prevented?

◆ Make sure the horse's schooling routine is varied.

◆ Make sure his feed does not have too high an energy content.

Calming feed supplements may prove useful, working on the premise that the cause must be treated rather than the symptom. In this case the aim would be to calm the horse's mind rather than to stop the bucking.

CAUSE On the surface it may appear that the horse has been scared, as many things invisible to us can frighten a horse. However, some are just naughty and will try to dislodge their rider or gain control. There may have been something alarming in a particular area once, but that does not mean the horse can run away every time he passes it.

Fortunately there are usually warning signs, though the rider must be tuned into his horse and learn to recognise them. He may tense up, raise his head, dip his quarters, or make snorting noises.

SOLUTION As soon as this happens the rider must make sure he is sitting firmly in the saddle, that his legs are secure and that he is driving the horse forwards. The reins must be short but not drastically so, as the rider must be able to turn the horse quickly before he takes a hold. If the horse recognises the term 'No!' as a chastisement for insolence, the rider will find this has an effect when combined with firm riding. The horse should be turned in a circle and calmed down, and made to walk quietly. Making progress past the offending area or object may take a while, and should be done gradually. It may be helpful to have someone lead the horse past, combined with calming and encouraging words from the rider; but it is unwise to dismount as the rider has more control on board.

SOLUTION One riding school horse the author has encountered would get to a certain point on a hack and would begin to walk backwards, ignoring all aids until he had reached his destination. This sort of pig-headedness must be stopped early on, as it will be a hard habit to break once the horse has lost respect for his rider. The only solution is firm riding and persistence, the rider taking a whip and even an assistant to lead the horse should he misbehave. It may be worthwhile playing the horse at his own game, and letting him stand still. A battle of wits is never productive, but may result in the horse getting bored first!

If the horse becomes rigid in traffic, he may well be frightened and awaiting instructions from his rider. In this instance he needs confidence and encouragement, and must be accustomed to riding out in traffic gradually. No matter how old the horse, he should be treated as an inexperienced youngster, and taken back to basics (see Traffic Shy, page 82).

Taking off

PROBLEM Some horses (perhaps those which are particularly intelligent?) display other evasive action when schooling, such as 'taking off' and shooting across the school or field. This may be a prelude to bolting; how can it be stopped?

Refusing to move

PROBLEM Some horses plant themselves firmly and may refuse to move at all; more commonly they want to return to their stable. How do you overcome this irritating habit?

Part 2:
SCHOOLING

Losing balance: 1

PROBLEM The process of schooling a young horse must be undertaken carefully, as a bad start can cause behaviour problems for the rest of his life. One of the first considerations when teaching the horse new procedures should be, how much can his natural balance and equilibrium affect his progress and development?

SOLUTION It is imperative that youngsters obtain a good sense of balance and rhythm, as throughout their adult life they will be asked to perform many tasks requiring 'a leg at each corner'; in fact, many of the problems associated with loss of balance are directly related to the horse's legs. Thus, if the carrying capacity is not equal in the hindquarters, the horse may well develop problems such as one-sidedness and stiffness. As with most humans, different horses have different weak spots. If the weakness is in the hindlegs (which provide the impulsion), the horse's rhythm will not be satisfactory and its balance will be affected. All youngsters should be given suppling exercises in the course of their schooling, particularly stretching work and transitions. It is important not to neglect one rein over the other, but to work on strengthening the weak spot. Working on a 20m circle to start with, decreasing and increasing its size encourages the inside hind leg to support the body, the rider using plenty of leg to maintain impulsion, taking care not to lean on the reins. The rider's position will also affect the horse's way of going, a lopsided seat putting more weight on one side of the horse than the other. Often it is all too easy for the rider to relax the inside shoulder and hip when circling, a habit which will impede correct movement and may cause stiffness. By raising the inside shoulder a little and making sure that the seatbones take equal weight, the rider can help to combat this problem.

One might imagine that the horse's centre of balance is in the centre of the saddle, but this is not so: it is in fact about a third of the way back along the body, just behind the shoulder and below the withers. It is this far forward because the horse's head is so heavy, so it is important to counterbalance its weight, and the weight of the rider, by encouraging strong forward action from the quarters. This is obtained largely by correct riding, using the leg to create impulsion, and a light contact so that the horse does not learn to lean on the rider's hand for support. Even when the head is stretched down, the hindquarters should maintain the same action and rhythm, and good posture and balanced riding should ensure this. Work without stirrups is always useful to assist the rider's balance, although this is not necessarily to be recommended on a young horse which is himself learning. An unbalanced rider will create an unbalanced horse.

Some people make their horses more supple to the left, albeit unwittingly; this is due to the way they handle them

Sit square (left)! How can the horse perform a rhythmic dressage test, or jump accurately, or avoid pecking on landing from, say, a drop fence, if you are slumped to one side (right)?

and school them initially, possibly because they are right-handed, allowing more play in their right hand and therefore permitting the right side of the horse's neck to stretch and develop more fully. If the near-side neck muscles are not equally developed, they will not stretch and so support the horse so well on the right rein, thus causing a 'pottery' action. This situation may be exacerbated by the practice of leading horses from the near side. In order to maintain equal bend and ultimately balance to the left and the right, riders must make sure that all exercises are carried out equally on both reins. If the rider's right hand is more flexible, a conscious effort should be made not to give extra play with those fingers.

If the horse still appears to be losing his balance, there is the possibility that there is a problem with his feet. The farrier can check whether or not there is a correct weight-bearing surface on each hoof, and will ensure that the toes are of the correct length. Attention must be paid to the feet on a regular basis, usually every six weeks.

The horse will find it very difficult to maintain his own balance and carry himself with 'ease and lightness' if the rider's bad position is upsetting it all the time: have an instructor check that you really are sitting up straight and square, with a straight line from your elbow to the horse's bit, and are not tipping forwards (left) or backwards (right).

Losing balance: 2

PROBLEM   Some horses tend to stumble and 'tip' their heads: how can this uncomfortable tendency be remedied?

SOLUTION   Sometimes a horse 'tips' his head when he loses his balance and stumbles. This is usually caused by one of two things: either he is trying to rebalance himself by poking out his nose, or he has been pulled in the mouth by an unseated rider and is wary of taking up a contact once more. The rider should gently take up a contact and maintain impulsion with the leg, supporting the horse and encouraging him forwards. He should be ready to give with the hands or slip the reins should the horse lose his balance again, preventing him being jabbed in the mouth.

Disunited in canter

PROBLEM Sometimes when a horse is very unbalanced in canter, the gait will become disunited. What exactly does this involve, and how can it be remedied?

The position slightly behind the girth that the rider's outside leg might assume when asking for canter strike-off, thus encouraging engagement of the horse's outside hind leg which should start the correct canter stride sequence.

When a horse becomes disunited, one of two things is happening: either the three-time rhythm has been broken to become a four-time rhythm, or the sequence of legs has changed. In a correct three-time canter the outside hind leads, with the inside hind and outside fore hitting the ground as a pair, followed by the inside fore. If the horse is slightly disunited, the diagonal pair may not hit the ground quite simultaneously. If he becomes totally unbalanced, the two outside legs may become the pair, in which case the sequence would be the inside hind, the outside hind and outside fore together, followed by the inside fore.

The main cause of a disunited canter is a generally unbalanced horse, and this is usually because the rider is asking more of him than he is capable of giving. If the horse is being schooled and educated in a methodical fashion, he will learn to trot when the walk is balanced, and to canter when the trot is balanced, and in order to canter properly he should have developed a good head carriage, and natural balance and rhythm. If this is not established, the power from the hindquarters will be insufficient to maintain quality forward movement, and the result will be trailing hindlegs and a disunited canter – and this way of going may well become a habit. Plenty of dedicated schooling is required to resolve this problem. Circle work will prove particularly useful because it engages the outside hind and encourages a good upward transition into canter.

In the first instance it *may* help if the rider lifts his weight off the horse's back throughout the transitions and canter. If the horse has never really used his quarters in canter, the muscles may be weak and under-developed; by taking the weight his back the transition may be made easier. Initially just a few strides are enough, providing the rider has brought the horse back to trot and not the other way round. As a guide, a good schooling session might consist of work on two 20m circles in a figure eight, using one circle to re-balance the trot and one to work in canter. The transitions can be asked for on different points of the circle to avoid the horse anticipating, gradually cantering for a few more strides each time. At this stage the maximum duration of the canter should not be more than half of the circle. Once the horse has accomplished acceptable transitions on both reins, half circles across the school or cantering large for a few strides can be attempted. The long side of the school is where most horses lose their balance, so extra support must be provided by the leg aids, and encouragement given for good work.

Lungeing with balancing reins may help to establish a good canter rhythm, as long as the horse does not race off or get excited. Once the quarter muscles develop and support the horse with ease he will be less likely to disunite, and the canter periods can be extended. However, it should always be the rider who decides when to go forwards to trot, and never the horse.

Just as humans are left- or right-handed, so horses are naturally less supple to one side than to the other, and therefore favour one bend more than the other. It is quite common to hear someone say 'this is his stiff side', or 'he favours the left/right rein'. In fact most horses seem to favour the left rein. Their canter work on the right rein may therefore require a little more patience, but it is important to devote as much time as may be necessary to this, as it is in the horse's best interest to be supple and balanced on both reins in order that he may more easily avoid injury from stumbling or slipping over. In order to avoid one-sidedness, those responsible for training the horse should guard against certain practices. For instance, it sometimes becomes a habit to walk into the schooling area in the same direction; if the gate is on the left-hand side, the natural reaction is to walk onto the outside track to the right. This means that the order of rein changes probably stays the same each time the horse is ridden, so perhaps he always finishes the session on the right rein; at this stage he is probably quite tired and may not be concentrating, and less will be accomplished on that rein. The same can be said of lungeing, as most people lead the horse into the school on the near side, naturally asking it to walk first to the left.

Canter corrections

PROBLEM
In canter many horses will always strike off on one particular leg, regardless of the rein they are on. Why is this, and what can be done to correct the problem?

SOLUTION
The accepted procedure for achieving a correct canter strike-off is to circle the horse on the left rein before asking for the left lead in canter, and on the right rein for the right lead. However, in order for the horse to be able to comply consistently, he must be well balanced, and he must have learnt to interpret the aids correctly for the movement. The rider must know how to apply these aids, and should already have mastered the 'feel' of when the horse is balanced and therefore ready to accept the aids. Striking off on the correct leg in canter is a fundamental part of

If the horse is a little sluggish to the rider's leg aids he may need a light flick with the schooling whip. The key is to strike off in canter with that leg leading. To this end, it is unhelpful to think of producing inside flexion; it is far better simply to think of keeping the horse straight, and only allow him to canter when he is in the correct balance for the correct lead.

many activities, not least dressage and showjumping, yet many riders do have great difficulty in achieving it; the correct procedure is therefore set out here in a step-by-step format.

1   First of all a steady rhythm in trot should be achieved and then maintained.

2   The rider should then indicate the required direction by establishing a more flexible contact and a slight bend; to do this he or she applies the fingers intermittently to the inside rein.

3   While sitting to the trot the rider then checks her position for the bend she is on by:
   - turning the shoulders slightly to the inside, thus following the bend of the horse;
   - bringing the inner seatbone forwards, transferring slightly more weight onto it, while maintaining an upright position.

The correct sequence of footfalls in canter can be seen clearly here: the horse is on the right rein with, therefore, the off-fore as the leading leg; so he pushes off with the near hind, then the near fore and the off-hind follow through and hit the ground together, whilst the off fore comes forwards and then strikes the ground alone. There is then actually a 'moment of suspension' when the horse has no feet on the ground at all; and then the sequence starts all over again.

4   The outside rein is used to control the impulsion, and to a degree the balance; however, it should follow the movement of the horse's head and neck while the rider's hand preserves a constant contact.

5   Impulsion is maintained by using both legs and a supple seat. However, the inside leg takes on a more dominant role in order to motivate the horse to bring his inside hindleg forwards and slightly under the centre of his body, so that he can follow the true line of the bend.

6   The outside leg is then applied behind the girth to induce the horse to bring his outside hind leg forwards and so start the sequence of the canter gait with the inside foreleg leading.

7   The rider's outside leg should remain in this position behind the girth throughout the canter in order to prevent the horse's hindquarters from swinging to the outside of the bend. By using and maintaining the above aids in canter, much of the impulsion which is generated by the rider's inside leg on the girth will be transferred diagonally

towards the outside shoulder, where it is controlled by the rider's non-restraining outside rein.

8   The inside rein should keep the horse's mouth soft and supple and indicate a slight bend to the inside.

Change and variety in the course of a schooling session are vital, so use plenty of changes of direction and spend adequate time on each rein. It could be that the horse which favours a particular canter lead has a lazy owner who leaves much to chance when asking for canter. It is a good idea to go back to basics, giving stronger aids and asking for the transition in a corner.; this will encourage inside bend and the correct strike-off. The horse could just be confused; or in the case of the more experienced animal where only subtle leg aids are required, he may just need a reminder of the precise aids! If this is not the case, try asking for the canter strike-off from a circle. First take the horse onto a 20m circle in trot; this alone will help engage the outside hind, and the smaller the circle, the harder it will be for him to take off on the wrong lead. Naturally it would be foolish to risk him stumbling or tripping by cantering in *too* small a circle, so immediately the canter is engaged, the rider should move to the outside track.

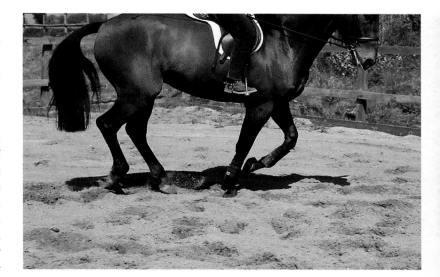

Using ground poles can prove very useful: place one in the corner of the school or on a circle, and ask for the canter transition so that the horse's first stride is over the pole – sliding the outside leg back a little further will emphasise the fact that the outside hind must be engaged. The pole can be raised for extra encouragement, and the exercise continued, going forwards into trot before approaching the pole again. The trot must be re-balanced before the approach each time, otherwise the horse may end up jumping the pole, getting faster and faster at each attempt. As the horse conveys that he understands what is required, the aids can be minimised once more so that they are subtle but precise. Plenty of transitions on a 20m circle should ensure the problem does not recur.

Working on the Bit

PROBLEM   Once the horse has established a good sense of rhythm and balance, the natural progression in his development should be a relaxed jaw and pleasing outline. However, some horses seem to find it difficult to work 'on the bit': so what exactly does this term mean, and how can the end result be achieved?

SOLUTION   Exactly what is required in working a horse 'on the bit' is probably one of the most misunderstood aspects of schooling and tuition. The desired outline ultimately requires a well schooled and willing horse, but unfortunately it seems that in the first instance many animals are bullied into submission and are made to lower their heads by aggressive riding. In order to work in a correct outline, the horse must be straight and balanced throughout the body; moreover he should have a relaxed head-carriage showing no resistance, and should move with plenty of impulsion generated from the hindquarters. In some ways the latter is the most important propensity, as without impulsion the horse will

Left A horse working nicely on the bit: a rounded topline, a soft acceptance of the bit, with the head near vertical but without any tenseness or too much shortening of the neck; and plenty of activity in the hock and hindquarters.

Right This horse could be rounder over his back and neck; this would make him soften in the rider's hand and more active in his hock and hindquarters. A classic case of the head being tucked in, but the quarters 'trailing out behind'.

not be energetically forward-going, he will be just poddling along on his forehand. From the observer's point of view, the end result of a correct outline is that the horse holds his head so that it is vertical to the ground. Unfortunately, many inexperienced riders think that just because the head is tucked in, the horse is 'on the bit'; this means that many horses are trudging along with their heads pulled in, but with their quarters trailing out behind, their riders oblivious to the fact that much more energy is required in order to engage the quarters.

So what should the rider do in order for the horse to go 'on the bit'? Assuming that the horse's programme of flatwork is satisfactory, it is a case of strong riding and still hands. If the hands move about and do not maintain a steady, even contact, the horse will have nothing to work forwards into, and will probably end up going faster and faster with his head in the air. A good way of practising the art of still hands is to hold onto a neckstrap whilst riding – most riders will be surprised at just how much their hands have been moving about. The leg aids need to be consistent and strong so the horse will be encouraged to respond to the impulsion indicated by the leg, and will work forwards and energetically into the rein contact. There should be a certain amount of play in the rider's fingers – though this must not develop into a sawing action – otherwise the horse may lean on the hand, in response to which the rider will shorten the reins and restrict the horse's movement. However, let it be said that all horses are different in conformation and temperament, so there can be no hard and fast rules, and no guarantee of a perfect outline straightaway. The best way to achieve results is to school in the presence of an instructor or an experienced friend, one who can see what is required and who may even ride the horse himself. Problems are often easier to spot from the ground, so it can be worth paying someone to help.

The horse which persistently resists and evades the contact requires a different approach. First it is important to be sure that it is not suffering any physical problems such as badly fitting tack, or back pain or sharp teeth; it may even be advisable to have the animal examined by a veterinary surgeon. Second, the horse's temperament must be considered – for instance, excitable or nervous horses are bound to be less co-operative when it is a question of schooling and discipline. Fortunately there are many calming products on the market nowadays, in the form of herbs and remedies, and these can often work wonders in relaxing the more excitable, highly strung horse.

There are also various schooling aids for use when the horse is being ridden: running reins (above) and draw reins (below) will help encourage him to stay round — though be careful he doesn't overbend and lean on the hand.

As far as schooling is concerned, the horse must be taken back to basics, because he cannot work properly and effectively without the carriage and balance we have described; lungeing may help to encourage this. There are also various schooling aids on the market for use when lungeing, some of which do help as they provide a contact for the horse to work into; but the person lungeing should be careful not to interfere or tug at the mouth while using them. The horse should be encouraged to stretch and to work in a long and low outline so the topline of the neck is relaxed and supple and can be developed.

Once the horse has established a good rhythm and is able to propel himself from behind with straightness and energy, the rider should work on transitions from the saddle; this will help the horse to bring his hocks underneath him, and so engage the hindquarters, his 'engine'. It is important that the rider maintains a sensitive contact with the hand at all times, restraining excess forward movement but not restricting the horse's action. School movements are useful, especially decreasing and increasing circles: as the horse flexes to the inside, the rider should soften the hand a little so that the horse learns that this is the most comfortable option in his way of going. However, it is again advised that for such an important part of the horse's education, an instructor is available to give help and guidance.

Overbending

PROBLEM In an effort to achieve a correct outline, some riders inadvertently encourage their horse to overbend, with the result that the head is tucked too much into the chest. How can this problem be resolved?

SOLUTION It must be emphasised at this point that overbending is a form of evasion. It may look like a pleasing outline to some people, but in reality the horse which tucks his head in is trying to avoid the contact as much as one that raises his head. Fortunately it is often quite easy to resolve, as most overbent horses are capable of producing more impulsion but without pulling at the rider's hands. From the rider's point of view, the horse drops the contact and the natural reaction is to shorten the reins; of course this in turn encourages it to bring its head in further, thus exacerbating the problem.

The horse must learn to work long and low, stretching his neck without running and gaining speed; he must be encouraged to stretch his head and neck at all gaits, and this can be given as a form of relaxation and a reward for hard work, along with a pat and some encouraging words (horses that have done a lot of driving or race-trotting find this mentally difficult, and may be cautious of stretching down for fear of punishment). School movements are useful, carried out with a loose rein contact but with plenty of impulsion; the rider may bring the hands away from the neck and down a little. Playing with the reins will also encourage the horse to stretch: just enough play to move the bit within the mouth a little, but not so much that the head is pulled to one side or the other. Once the horse will move willingly at a consistent pace, the reins can be gradually taken up. At all times the leg aids must be strong and consistent so the hocks propel the horse into the rider's hand; it may help in understanding what is required if the rider can envisage containing the impulsion in the hand rather than simply slowing the pace. Eventually the reins can be shortened to a reasonable length, although the rider must always be careful to keep the contact light and the hands still because if the horse feels restrained he may feel compelled to resort to his old tactic.

If the horse's head is tucked in by even a little too much past the vertical (above), his shoulder movement will tend to be restricted and his back tense and he will find it hard to engage his back end. Encourage him therefore to work 'long and low' (right).

Falling in on the circle

SOLUTION Often the horse which falls in with his quarters will compensate by dropping the outside shoulder, which indicates stiffness. By the same token if the inside shoulder drops in on the circle, the quarters may swing out, so the horse is almost working in a series of straight lines rather than supporting himself and bending correctly. The rider must work on the horse's stiffness and lack of obedience, and once he has improved in this field, he will learn to respond to the rider's inside leg. The problem probably stems from the horse's back, so exercises encouraging the hocks to work harder and the horse to bend and stretch throughout his whole body will help.

A series of school exercises in the form of a training plan may be drawn up, to work certain areas in succession and on both reins. For instance, you may begin by walking the horse large on a long rein, making sure you are using firm leg aids and supporting him around the corners. A line of cones or small oil drums may be laid out, set far enough apart so that it is relatively easy for the horse to bend around them in walk. The reins may be brought away from the neck slightly at this stage, using an open hand to guide the horse. The cones may then be brought closer together, and the horse's reins taken up as he progresses, with the rider maintaining firm leg aids and sliding the outside leg back a little to support the quarters.

Any circling exercises, in walk and then in trot, will prove useful. The circles may be decreased and increased in size, the rider keeping a soft contact and the legs working hard to maintain impulsion and support the horse. Small circles in walk with the horse's neck bent to the inside will stretch the muscles, with the outside leg taken back a little and the weight evenly distributed on the saddle.

Pole work will encourage the horse to use his back, and may be done in walk, trot and canter. Lungeing will also prove beneficial, particularly without a rider so the horse may be observed working without intervention. Using a balancing rein may help the horse to find his own carriage and improve his rhythm once he has established a good sense of balance.

Once these exercises have been carried out daily for a few weeks, riders may attempt lateral movements, including leg-yielding. This can be carried out both on a circle and along a straight side, and should improve the horse's responsiveness. Once the horse has improved sufficiently he should be more obedient and responsive to the leg, so riders must maintain correct riding and suppling exercises in the course of their schooling, to prevent the problem re-occurring.

PROBLEM Falling in occurs frequently both under saddle and on the lunge, and is a sign of a lack of training. A horse which is supple and obedient is unlikely to fall in on a circle, as he will be tracking up correctly, his hind feet falling in the tracks left by the front feet. How can you stop the horse falling in?

Place the poles fanlike on the ground with the inside ends at a walk distance apart, the middle at trot and the outside ends suitable for a canter stride (a). Raising one end of the poles on blocks (b) will encourage much greater activity; this is also extremely tiring for the horse, however, so never overdo such an exercise – 10 minutes would probably be plenty.

Excitability

PROBLEM Some horses seem naturally high-spirited, spooking and shying at just about anything in their path. Why are some animals more excitable than others, and what calming measures can be taken?

(top) Sugar beet and (above) flaked maize: both are high energy feeds, so if your horse is not in hard work he won't need too much of these; otherwise you risk making him excitable and spooky!

SOLUTION As humans are different, so are horses and their personalities, their temperaments and moods can vary widely: whilst some are placid and extremely willing, others are full of nervous tension, making their riders feel as if they are sitting on an unexploded bomb. The reasons which lie behind excess energy or excitement are numerous, and not always easy to pinpoint. Some breeds are more highly strung than others – for instance, Arabs and Thoroughbreds tend to be more excitable than native breeds and cobs – and there is little that can be done about breed characteristics. However, some preventative measures can be taken to minimise excessive energy. First, the horse's diet must be considered. Foods that are high in carbohydrate, such as oats and maize, must only be given to the horse in hard work that has the opportunity to burn up the energy. Also, foods high in sugar may have an energising effect; thus a diet containing both sugar beet pulp and molasses may have to be altered, as the two may exceed the daily sugar requirements. The owner who is unsure of the energy requirements of his horse should seek expert advice; for a small fee, an equine nutritionist will advise on a suitable diet, and can be contacted via most feed manufacturers.

Excitable behaviour is not always caused by high spirits; in fact there are many cases where it is a manifestation of pain – for instance if the horse has back problems he may try to escape the discomfort by bolting or leaping. If the excitement is always associated with a certain school manoeuvre or transition, then this is a likely cause. The horse's tack should be checked by a professional, and changed if deemed unsuitable. A physical check-up should also be made by a vet or equine physiotherapist, to ensure that there is no long-term medical problem.

The next step might be to try natural remedies; these are available from most manufacturers in ready-mixed forms, or can be home-grown, or bought as herbs and plants. The manufactured preparations are often given in powdered or ground form and give pleasing results, being mixed into the feed on a daily basis; and in liquid form they can be added to drinking water. These supplements usually contain the processed versions of their natural counterparts, such as camomile, hops and brewers' yeast; they are carefully measured to give precise amounts, and as such are easy and practical. However, their one disadvantage is that they can prove expensive, and at least if owners prepare their own remedies there is less chance of overdosing by inadvertently feeding too much at any one time.

A last resort is to consult a veterinary surgeon with regard to obtaining sedatives. These are not a long-term answer, but can be useful in certain situations. Some horses may be prescribed a short-term course of sedatives in order to recover from a psychological problem; in such cases they are very useful, providing these horses are weaned off them slowly.

Napping and shying

SOLUTION Some horses are naturally more 'spooky' than others and are clearly of a nervous nature. This may be influenced by breed characteristics, but will depend on the general character and willingness of the horse.

PROBLEM Napping or shying occurs when a horse is seemingly scared of an object or area, and suddenly leaps sideways in haste. How can you tell if there is real cause for concern?

The rider may see a pattern emerging: some horses are scared of certain smells and may, for instance, shy every time they hack past a farm. Perhaps there is a certain colour that affects them? Even though horses in theory can only see in black or white, research shows that certain colours of the spectrum affect horses more than others. Certainly some horses are fearful of white, but this is probably because the sunlight makes it appear brighter.

If there is something specific the horse is scared of, the obvious step is to accustom him to it gradually. Thus the horse which is scared of the smell of a farm, perhaps associating it with a previous incident, should be ridden past one every day. A horse scared of white jumps may be schooled and fed alongside the equipment, until it is no longer an issue.

However, many nappy horses simply lack confidence in themselves, in the same way as someone who is scared of the dark. Once their level of confidence has increased, the foe does not seem so bad and can be overcome. Thus the rider must encourage rather than chastise the horse, riding him firmly past the object rather than smacking him when he is already worked up. It is usually possible to tell the difference between a genuinely frightened horse and one which is 'trying it on'; if he is playing a game and testing his rider, a workmanlike attitude and an encouraging tone will soon sort him out.

If the horse's temperament seems to blame, and he is very nervous of everything, it may be necessary to adjust his diet (see Excitability p60).

If all else fails, it may be as well to avoid certain objects or areas if the horse naps at them repeatedly and is irrationally scared. Though this may be seen as giving in to the horse or giving up, it may be the most sensible course of action in the long run. After all, the horse's psyche is largely understood, and deep-rooted fears may never be conquered. It may be safest to take an alternative route if a battle always ensues in the middle of a particular road, and lives are endangered. The individual situation must be assessed, and riders must act upon their common sense.

Keep behind the movement if the horse naps and runs backwards; you want him to go forwards, so don't keep pulling and tugging at his mouth – try to maintain a light, even contact, but be very firm with your seat and leg aids. The same applies with a horse that shies; and remember that shoulder-in is a useful exercise when trying to persuade a horse past something he finds frightening or spooky.

Head shaking

PROBLEM Head shaking is a problem with various causes. In effect it breaks the rider's rein contact and makes schooling very difficult. So where might it have originated, and what can be done to cure it?

SOLUTION Head shaking is fairly common, so let us investigate the circumstances which might cause it. For instance, many horses are quite excitable when first ridden, just as the wind under their tail, or the sight of a companion may often lead to head tossing and squealing – but to this degree it is quite acceptable, and not necessarily a long-term problem. On the other hand, the horse may be cleverly evading the contact by changing the position of his head so the rider's hands cannot be kept still, and this could become a more long-standing problem. It could be caused by a heavy-handed rider who perhaps jabs at the corners of the mouth or leans on the reins. It is important to keep light, still hands, as once the horse's mouth is sore he may always resent the contact.

It is possible that the bridle is uncomfortable; perhaps the bit is pinching the lips, or the browband is too tight. Sores present around the head will be very painful if chafed by tack, so it is a good idea to examine the horse's head with the bridle both on and off. Particular attention should be paid to hairy areas, as they may conceal sores or scabs.

The answer may be a simple one, in that flies or wind are annoying the horse. The noise of buzzing or the irritation of insects near the ears will send some horses into a frenzy, and a strong wind will cause most horses to duck their heads. Fitting a fly fringe with ears may help to resolve this problem, whether in summer or winter.

A common cause of head shaking is something actually *in* the ears, such as ear mites. A physical examination will determine this, though headshy horses may need restraining if the pain or irritation is great. The veterinary surgeon will provide appropriate medication or suggest a course of action.

Once you have established and resolved the cause of the head shaking, the horse may suddenly stop this behaviour and become a pleasure to school. Unfortunately horses learn habits quickly, and old ones die hard, and he may therefore continue the 'game' even though the cause has been resolved. In this instance he must be schooled with a very light rein contact, using plenty of leg to prevent him dropping on the forehand; once the hocks are propelling him forward, he may be more inclined to keep a steadier contact. However, it may be necessary to start the schooling from scratch, as if the horse were overbent (see page 58).

A fly fringe with ears, a boon for those horses which headshake because of flies or wind. Such fringes are permitted in showjumping competitions, but not, however, in any dressage competitions.

Crossing the jaw

SOLUTION Crossing the jaw and opening the mouth are simple but effective evasions, generally caused by discomfort or pain; moreover the pain could realistically be located in several places, not just in the horse's mouth, which is the first and most obvious place to look. For instance, the bit could be ill-fitting, perhaps pinching the tongue or hitting the horse's teeth; or it may be too heavy – some horses prefer a lightweight, hollow bit if they are fussy or sensitive. The pain could be caused by an ill-fitting bridle, and just a few simple adjustments could resolve the problem. Sore areas within the mouth might be to blame, perhaps caused by ulcers or sharp teeth; a vet or equine dentist will be able to confirm this, and to recommend appropriate action. Those riders who believe it is the bit at fault would be wise to eliminate all other areas before changing the type of bit.

PROBLEM Why do some horses constantly attempt to cross their jaw or open their mouth? What causes this action, and how can the problem be resolved?

Any part of the horse's body used for carrying weight or providing impulsion could affect the contact, and ultimately the horse's mouth – though it is more likely that lack of balance or stiffness are the cause, rather than physical problems, as any long-term physical problem will probably cause more than crossing of the jaw. Weak, inadequate hocks may cause evasion, as will leaning on the rider's hands. The horse which is heavily on the forehand may have a rider who attempts to lift the head the whole time, inadvertently causing it to resist.

Asking too much of the horse during a schooling session may cause evasion, for instance expecting him to perform a tight circle when his body is not yet supple enough. All schooling must be taken slowly and systematically, without asking for a correct outline until the jaw crossing or mouth opening has been resolved. Once the horse has established a balanced way of going with no discomfort, he should relax the head in response.

Unfortunately, some horses make crossing the jaw or opening the mouth a habit, whatever the cause. A noseband such as a grakle or flash will deter the horse from his habit, although these should only be used if there is no other obvious cause. Once the horse has established a pleasing outline and is balanced, these may be changed to a simple cavesson, and the grakle or flash only used for those occasions when the horse is likely to resort to old habits, when he is excited, for instance.

Hopping into trot

PROBLEM Sometimes when going forwards into trot, a horse will develop a little hop before the transition. This is uncomfortable for the rider, and it is also unsightly; so what could be the problem, and how can the horse be re-educated?

Transitions within the canter will also help the 'hopping' problem, as long as the aids are applied in the same way as in trot: this sort of work is excellent for encouraging engagement and thus improving the paces overall.

SOLUTION Hopping into trot is almost always caused by poor balance, the hindquarters not working hard enough to push the walk into a trot. This in turn is invariably caused by bad riding, the rider restricting the forward movement with the hands, but asking for a transition with the legs. Lungeing the horse through transitions will give an idea of where the problem lies: if the horse is fine without a rider, then the rider's skills must be addressed.

Be sure there is no physical discomfort: any lameness or sign of pain is generally easier to spot from the ground, and the horse's expression can be noted, too: perhaps a nerve is being trapped along the vertebrae, or there is a problem within the hindlegs or feet. The horse may be better on one rein than the other, which might suggest that it hurts him to take weight on a particular limb. Of course these problems can really only be verified by a veterinary examination.

If there is no physical reason for the hopping, then you must concentrate on correct, precise riding to cure the problem. It is important not to let the horse drop onto the forehand before the transition, but to keep a strong seat with firm leg aids and light hands. If the reins are too short the horse will be restricted, and may be receiving contrasting messages from the rider. Trot work involving lengthening and shortening of the strides may help, because if the hindleg action is pottery, longer flowing strides will help to loosen up the quarters. Use the long side of the schooling area to achieve this: the leg aids should be kept quiet and consistent, encouraging forward movement, and the pace can be checked when necessary with the outside rein. On reaching the short side of the school the stride can be shortened and re-bal-

anced, so the horse's normal working trot is established before the next set of lengthened strides.

It is important to free the quarters and create impulsion without speeding up the pace. As with the problems discussed regarding the canter strike-off, plenty of transitions will help, going from halt to walk to trot and back down again, with only five to ten strides in between. Riding these manoeuvres on a circle may assist with balance problems, too, and encourage engagement of the hocks. Repetition is an excellent schooling aid and horses always learn from it, providing it is maintained!

If riders continue to experience the same problems with their horses following examination by the vet and stringent schooling, then the cause may be stiffness in the joints. However, there are various natural feed supplements available to combat this, including comfrey and kelp. Oil-based supplements such as cod-liver oil are widely used, and can be found with other supplements at feed manufacturers and tack shops.

Hollowness

PROBLEM

Why do some horses work in such a hollow shape – is it due to conformation, or incorrect schooling? What can be done to re-educate the horse, and how can hollowness be prevented in the future?

SOLUTION

Far too many horses work in a tight, hollow outline. This is generally caused by bad training, and it may refer right back to the time when the horse was broken in. This is the point in its life when the muscles are starting to build into a certain shape, and once it is used to working in a certain fashion, it will take great effort and dedication from both horse and rider to change that physique. To a certain extent the horse's natural conformation can play a part – thus long-backed horses with a high headcarriage are more likely to become established in this hollow shape without correct schooling, and will much more readily gain a weak back and an under-muscled topline. This is not to say that all Arabs, for instance, are hollow; it is just that if a horse doesn't have an ideal shape to begin with, it will require careful schooling to develop the correct muscles.

The hollow horse usually has a tight back, which instead of being relaxed is tense and inactive; the hocks may not be quite underneath the quarters, and the neck is often raised and stiff. In particular riders will notice the problem on a circle, as its quarters may swing out, the general shape of the school movement being more square than round. This may have been made worse by too much hacking, since the horse is then generally allowed to go along in a straight line and rarely bends; few riders school and work their horse on the bit whilst out hacking, so it is used to maintaining its own headcarriage.

Hollowness may also be made worse by inexperienced riders being left to gain experience on a willing and well behaved horse. Many of the kindest riding-school horses seem the worst schooled, as their beginner riders learn from their mistakes before progressing to more difficult mounts.

The horse with a hollow outline needs to be completely re-schooled in order to develop a long, low profile and a good topline, particularly along the crest of the neck and the loins. The hocks must engage properly, and the horse's back should be supple and relaxed. This is most easily achieved on the lunge, as are many school-

A Market Harborough in use. To encourage the horse to carry his head even lower the martingale clips can be attached to the third ring on the reins (the one closest to the rider's hands); to reduce the lowering effect, the first ring can be used (closest to the bit ring).

ing objectives. The horse will find it easier to work without the rider, and from the ground it is easier to see exactly what the problem is. He should be schooled without his saddle initially, perhaps using just a roller and bridle. He may find it difficult to describe circles at first, so they must be kept to around 20m; it may also be a while before his head and neck relax, so in the meantime, gentle transitions to supple and encourage free movement of the joints are in order.

Once the horse is comfortable on the lunge, some riders may wish to introduce a schooling aid such as a balancing rein; these can be very effective when the horse is on the lunge, providing they are correctly fitted and used. They allow correct muscle development without rider intervention, so the horse is more able to adjust his balance and maintain his forward movement once the rider's weight is added. Most

Draw-reins can also be used as a schooling aid; they can, however, tend to pull the horse too much onto his forehand if the rider is not sufficiently strong in the leg.

schooling aids only come into effect when the horse is in the wrong position; for instance, those that work on the horse's poll do so only when the head is raised above a desirable point. Most manufacturers produce their own versions, so interested riders should seek advice from riding instructors or experienced friends.

If a schooling aid is not an option (either due to cost, or a disbelief in their effectiveness), the answer lies in schooling, schooling and more schooling! Once the horse has been lunged and becomes a little more relaxed on the circle, riders can mount once more, and resume work in the school. Circles and school movements are essential, with plenty of transitions. The horse must be encouraged to work in a long and low shape, the rider allowing him to stretch the neck every so often. Bending around obstacles such as cones will help, making sure that work is carried out equally on both reins. Rider exercises include riding without stirrups to develop a good seat, and holding a neckstrap in conjunction with the reins to ensure still hands. Once the horse progresses, the rider must maintain a good seat and position, with strong leg aids and a varied schooling programme.

Laziness

PROBLEM The struggle some riders have to make their lazy horses work is exhausting to watch, let alone to have to put up with yourself! Nagging horses into reluctant submission is commonplace, but what is the cause of this unwillingness, and how can it be treated?

SOLUTION Some horses are just lazy and idle in character, as are some humans – they seem to have lower expectations of life and are happy doing as little as possible. In some ways breed characteristics may influence a horse's outlook, as fine, highly strung animals such as the Thoroughbred or the Arab are often more enthusiastic than the heavier, more commonly bred type such as the cob or Cleveland Bay.

A common cause for apparent laziness is boredom, often seen in riding school horses which may spend the best part of their day going round in circles. School work should therefore be continually varied to include jumping, pole work and bending. Transition work asks more of the horse, particularly the more demanding ones such as halt to trot, canter to walk, and walk to canter; these should wake him up and give him something to think about. The rider will need a great deal of enthusiasm himself to induce interest from the horse, and a vigorous warm-up should get schooling sessions off to a good start. A good, forward-going rhythm must be maintained at all times, so the horse is never given the opportunity to drag himself along or be lazy.

Carrying a whip is useful if it is applied sparingly, as nagging aids, whether they be from the leg or a whip, will become irritating to the horse and consequently ignored. Sometimes just the sight of the whip is enough to inspire life into a horse – although he should not become scared of it at any stage. Even so, a short, sharp smack when the horse really will not listen will be much more effective than endless leg aids, and the whip can be carried as a warning of future use.

Beware of mistaking ignorance for lack of enthusiasm, particularly in young horses which may not fully understand what is being asked of them. During the early schooling stages it is important to use plenty of voice aids in addition to leg aids to establish what is required. New tasks should be taught slowly and consistently, making sure the horse understands one task before moving on to another.

The horse which is consistently lazy may be suffering from pain or an ailment, and may be soldiering on because he is of a willing nature; some horses will continue to work even when in pain, so a physical problem may go unnoticed at the time. These problems are usually discovered in the future when weak spots develop, or old injuries surface under strain. Fortunately most horses are not so tolerant and will show by lameness or lethargy when they are in pain or ill. Nevertheless, it is up to the rider or owner to notice mood changes, as these are often indicative of an ailment: for instance kicking, bucking or excessive behaviour which is patently out of character often indicates a problem; and a placid horse may just become increasingly lethargic and generally unwilling to co-operate. If there are no obvious physical reasons for this, the vet may need to take a blood test to determine if the horse *is* suffering from certain ailments. Note, too, that respiratory or heart problems may cause a horse to become lethargic, and should always be considered if being lazy is out of character.

Take your lazy pony gymkhana racing! The competitive excitement of gymkhana games should rouse the adrenalin of even the most phlegmatic character.

On the forehand

PROBLEM Why do some horses persist in going along on the forehand – is this the fault of the rider, or is it because of the horse's conformation? What can be done to remedy the situation?

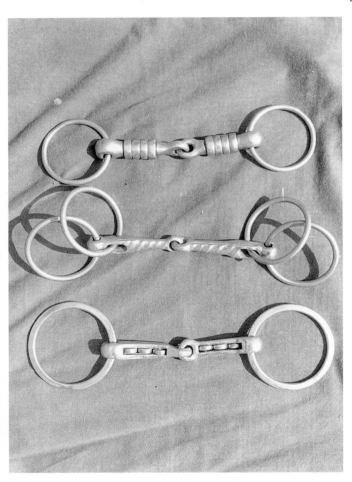

Loose-ring snaffles and bits with a rollered mouthpiece will discourage the horse from leaning on the hand.

SOLUTION A horse is considered to be on the forehand when his weight is distributed towards his front end, so that he leans on the rider's hand or pulls himself along without impulsion. If the rider's centre of balance is placed too far forwards, through tipping his body or pushing the legs forwards, the horse will respond by lowering or raising the head to re-balance himself. As the head is so heavy, the weight is taken on the forehand, so the hindquarters trail and the horse leans on the reins to support himself. To a certain extent conformation can play a part, and this should be taken into account whilst the horse is being trained – although there are probably just as many slightly built horses with lean necks on the forehand, as there are cobs with thick necks and large heads! Therefore a certain amount of fault may be the rider's, who should at all times sit deep in the saddle, with a secure seat and a straight back. The contact must be quite light, so the horse cannot lean on the rein and start a pulling contest. A bit with a fixed mouthpiece may give him something to get hold of, so a jointed mouthpiece may prove more beneficial, because it allows movement within the mouth. Bits with rollered mouthpieces are also useful, and will give the horse something else to think about.

This is all right if the horse is reasonably obedient, but some horses on the forehand also pull, in which case riding with only a light contact and using a mild bit may just give them an excuse to go faster; for these a more drastic approach may be needed. A stronger bit may be used for a short while – though in knowledgeable hands – to solve the problem of maintaining a light contact but without the horse being able to pull. It is far better to school temporarily in a stronger bit – the restraining capacity used in experienced hands – than to spend a long while fighting the horse using a mild bit. Once the horse's balance has improved, and when the muscles have correctly re-developed and the carriage has been lifted, a milder bit can be re-introduced.

Transition work with the rider's hands slightly raised may help, keeping them still with a light contact. The horse must learn to develop his own balance, with the hocks driving forwards and the head in a correct outline. A balancing rein may be used to help him find his natural carriage, at first on the lunge and then with a rider. Only a mild bit should be used in conjunction with any gadget, and it is wise to have an instructor or a knowledgeable assistant on the ground when using balancing reins, particularly for the first time. Once the horse's capacity for carrying weight correctly has improved, he will be better able to tackle ground poles or jumps without tripping up or refusing.

Jogging

PROBLEM One of the most exasperating experiences for a rider is hacking out a horse which continually jogs, instead of walks. This is a very bad habit, and most uncomfortable for the rider. So what causes jogging, and how can it be remedied?

SOLUTION The two predominant causes of jogging are excitement and anticipation. We all know that before or during an important event we often get excited, an emotion particularly apparent in children. Horses are just the same, and they too will produce excess nervous energy which in some cases is expressed as jogging. The excitability generally arises when an event or happening is not part of the horse's regular routine, for instance the monthly visit to a showjumping course, or a weekly hack. Since these events occur less frequently than his other, perhaps monotonously regular activities, and if he enjoys what is happening, then he probably becomes all the more excited. In order to overcome this sort of excitability it is important to provide variety to the horse's schooling sessions, popping over a crosspole unexpectedly or ending the session with a light hack. Once events that he would normally consider exciting become commonplace or at least more frequent, the horse may calm down and take them in his stride.

Anticipation often occurs when the horse is learning something, and he is being asked to practise certain movements over and over again. This might apply if the rider is practising for instance for a dressage test; the horse will learn the test off 'pat' as well, and once he knows what is coming next, he may perform the movements automatically, anticipating the faster paces by jogging. In some ways it is good that he is willing to please, but this sort of anticipation may become a habit and ultimately lead to inattentiveness. Again, variety should be included to break a monotonous routine. As far as the rider is concerned, his aids must be made clear so there is no confusion on the horse's part; and the horse must learn to respect the rider and to wait for the commands and aids. Much of his schooling should be done in walk, so he learns to relax and stride out. Transitions will help, always varying the number of strides in between gaits.

The rider should keep a very deep seat, driving the horse forwards at all times. It is no good just trying to slow down the pace with the hand, because the horse will often simply jog on the spot; the impulsion must be utilised to go forwards rather than up and down, and to do this a strong leg and a still hand are necessary, combined with patience. While it may be very tempting to jab the horse in the mouth and shout, this really only serves to make the rider feel better. Occasionally a sharp check with the rein may help if the horse refuses to listen, though this should only be administered when truly necessary. Also, the rider must be careful not to take up the reins suddenly, because this is often a signal for faster work in the horse's mind! Practising lengthening and shortening the reins at the walk will be beneficial, reprimanding the horse every time he jogs or breaks into a trot, and praising him when the walk is consistent.

Calming supplements are available which can be added to the horse's feed if he persists in getting very excited, the dose being raised before a show or an event (though be careful not to exceed manufacturers' recommendations). A good tip is to feed plenty of camomile tea two days beforehand.

Straightness

PROBLEM Some horses find it difficult to maintain straightness, swinging their quarters out and causing their rider to lose control. How does this problem arise, and what methods can be used to remedy it?

Groundpoles can be used to encourage the horse to stay straight: start with a line of three or four poles parallel to, and about 2m away from the straight side of your schooling area; then to help him not wobble in the open, try two lines of poles 2m apart down the centre of the school.

SOLUTION The term 'straightness' is quite misleading, as it implies that the horse must be going in a straight line. In fact what it means is that the horse's body should follow the line of the track he is on, whether curved or straight, and the hind feet should follow the tracks of the front feet so that only two sets of tracks are seen as impressions in the ground. The horse which is using its quarters and has sufficient impulsion is said to be 'tracking up': that is, the hind feet fall directly into the tracks of the front feet, or even exceed the distance. A lack of impulsion may be partly to blame for a lack of straightness, as can immaturity on the horse's part, or poor riding. In a similar way to riding a bike, the less the propulsion from the pedals, the harder it is to keep the bike from wobbling – the handlebars may need to twist one way or another to compensate for the lack of forward motion. So lack of impulsion can lead directly to lack of balance when riding the horse, and plenty of leg is needed to create forward movement and to provide support. Also, remember that all young horses are wobbly in the first stages of their training, and need time to gain their balance and learn what is required.

Because much initial ridden training is done on the lunge or on circles, the horse will be used to relying on the rider's strong inside leg to bend around, and also a supportive outside leg. When he is ridden in a straight line, however, both of the rider's leg aids are equal, and this may confuse him. Should this be the case, the rider must keep the aids very firm and precise, allowing the horse to become accustomed to them, and to accept them. Swinging the quarters out indicates a good deal of stiffness, rather like trying to bend a plastic ruler which always snaps back into its original shape. The horse is unlikely to be bending properly around the rider's inside leg, and will not be tracking up; inspect his tracks on the ground and you will probably be able to see three or even four separate tracks. During re-schooling the horse will need to perform frequent suppling exercises to gain flexibility – bending around cones, and riding 15–20m circles will help, as long as the hocks are encouraged to provide impulsion with plenty of firm riding: the rider's outside leg should slide back as the horse bends, to prevent the quarters from swinging, and the inside hand should encourage bend, though without turning the neck into the circle. Once the quarters stay on the same track as the forehand – ie straight – on the circle, then the long sides and centre line of the school can be attempted, the rider's legs ready to slide back and push the quarters over should they begin to swing.

If the school has a surrounding fence or railing, the horse may learn to rely on it for guidance – in which case, frequent changes of rein across the school and varied movements should help to maintain his concentration. As with many schooling problems, transitions are useful, combined with strong riding and plenty of perseverance.

Clumsiness

SOLUTION Some horses do seem to be physically ungainly, while others possess the presence and grace fit for a gymnast. To a certain degree this may be due to the horse's make-up, as some are naturally more clumsy than others, just as we are. Most young horses are ungainly; one has only to watch a foal gambolling about to witness this, though this trait is usually outgrown in time. But whilst bones and muscles are still developing, it is usual for one end of the horse to grow more quickly than the other so that either the rump or the withers at some stage of growth is higher. However, by the time he is physically mature enough to ride, he should be quite level and will almost certainly be better co-ordinated.

Weakness in the limbs may cause tripping, as in the human ankle which may twist more readily as a result of previous injury. Unfortunately, weak areas in the young horse tend to stay vulnerable for a long period, though modern medicine is working wonders for certain ailments. Thus it is important not to 'push' youngsters by asking them to do a lot of work before their body and limbs are sufficiently mature, because injury acquired early in life may recur later on.

Foot-associated problems most commonly cause tripping, though generally these may be remedied by a visit from the farrier; long toes, for instance, may cause stumbling, though the problem is obviated if the horse's feet are shod or trimmed regularly. More serious would be internal disease of the foot, such as navicular disease. Once tripping and stumbling has become a confirmed problem, and if it is not thought to be caused by laziness or youth, the farrier or vet should examine the horse as soon as possible. And if physical causes are ruled out, then the horse will possibly need corrective shoeing in order to re-balance the hoof/pastern axis and so help him to balance himself and move more easily. The tripping may only occur when he is tired or lazy, so it is the owner's responsibility to make sure his hooves are in optimum shape and balance at all times.

In addition, the horse may be re-schooled in the same way as if he were on the forehand (see page 70), so he does not lean forwards or put undue strain on the front limbs. A slight reprimand when he stumbles may make him pick his feet up a little, combined with a check on the rein and a squeeze with the leg, to lift his head up; however, on *no* account should this be a jab in the mouth, as this will only cause him to lose his balance again. Riders should also make sure that the schooling area is flat, with no buried objects such as roots or stones which may be kicked up to the surface. As a precaution, knee boots should be used when hacking, just in case the horse stumbles on the road and comes down on his knees.

PROBLEM Why are some horses seemingly clumsy, tripping over their own feet and stumbling all the time? Is there a medical reason for this, or is the horse just unco-ordinated?

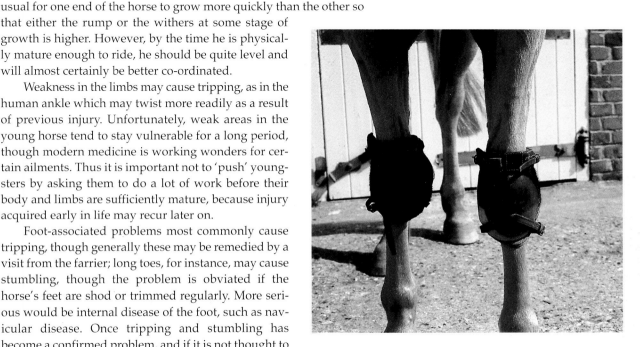

Kneeboots should always be worn if the horse is clumsy; these are available in leather, as shown here, but also in plastic fabric with Velcro attachment, which are cheaper.

Stargazing

PROBLEM Why do some horses adopt the stargazer position, their heads raised skywards and their necks very tense? It is annoying for the rider and potentially dangerous for both parties, so how can the situation be resolved?

SOLUTION Stargazing is an exaggerated form of being above the bit, and is notoriously difficult to cure unless the rider can dedicate a lot of time and patience to the problem. Moreover the older the horse, probably the more established the posture; initially there was no doubt good reason for the reaction, but over a period of time it may well have become a habit. And of course if the problem is of long standing, the muscles will have learned to support the neck in the raised position, so it will be uncomfortable for the horse to work normally. It is possible that an old or existing back problem may be the cause, though for the horse to react so violently it must have been – or must be – quite serious. A vet or back specialist will investigate the horse's physical health, and will suggest a course of action.

If the horse is found to be quite healthy, the evasion may initially have been caused by problems within the mouth, perhaps sharp teeth or an ill-fitting bit, or poor riding with severe use of the rein. The rider who constantly jabs the horse in the mouth as punishment is bound to cause him to raise his head, as he will always flinch in response to the rein contact. And if such treatment continues for a long period of time, the horse may choose to keep his head in the flinch position, thus keeping his mouth out of the way of such discomfort. Usually the rider will not recognise his mistake, and may sell on the horse, branding it as temperamental. Thus the horse's new rider, who is in no way responsible for the problem, is unavoidably confronted with its outcome, and will have a difficult job on his hands.

Firstly, it is safer to stay off the roads until the problem is at least partially resolved. Stargazing usually goes hand in hand with anxiety,

besides which the horse will have restricted vision, and this is obviously dangerous where there is traffic. Secondly, the rider must appreciate that in order to re-school the horse, a good deal of time will be required for the muscles to re-develop correctly: this is no short-term cure. It is wise to work with an instructor or an experienced friend who can help and advise from the ground, as this situation must be handled carefully. A very light contact must be used, in conjunction with a mild bit which is comfortable and correctly fitted.

The horse may be schooled, but only lightly, and work on the lunge is particularly advantageous because then the horse is not restricted in any way by the reins. He must be encouraged to stretch down, even though he may find it uncomfortable. When ridden, work in walk and trot will suffice to begin with, at all times keeping just a light contact. The horse will probably raise his head during transitions, so the rider must use his seat, leg and voice aids to make a downward transition. Rein contact should only be taken up very gradually, and only once the horse will work on a long rein with a relaxed head and neck. If, when the contact is taken up, the horse adopts his raised head position again, the rider must resume the exercise from the beginning; so progress can only be gradual.

There are some balancing reins which may prove useful, particularly if the problem is not resolved after careful schooling. Most suitable are those reins that allow stretching, but are uncomfortable when the head is raised; however, they may not be deemed appropriate by some riders. Even so, with remedial schooling and a patient rider there should be no reason for the stargazing problem to continue, though it will take plenty of time and effort.

Consistent and steady work over trotting poles should help to lower a stargazer's head carriage. This horse is still carrying his head too high and is obviously excited, but the repetitive nature of this sort of work will help to relax him and so encourage him to develop a longer, lower outline.

Bolting

PROBLEM The horse that bolts is both unpredictable and dangerous; so what are the causes of this behaviour, and what can be done to prevent it happening again?

Realistically speaking, it is not worth persevering with the confirmed bolter, as sooner or later one accident will prove fatal. Owners must make their own decision as to the future of such a horse, but they should always remember that bolting is a vice which is rarely curable.

SOLUTION Being bolted with is truly one of the most frightening experiences imaginable: a passenger on board a strong and often scared animal, you are totally out of control and galloping blindly. There is usually an element of fear involved: perhaps a bird flew out in front of the horse, or maybe he was bitten by a dog or a snake. Pain could be a factor, but it usually only causes the initial fear – the horse in severe pain will probably not continue to bolt. Most scared animals take refuge in flight, but it may be possible to slow the horse in the early stages of his 'escape', before he takes hold and speeds up.

If the horse has not been scared and is simply misbehaving, then such behaviour is unforgivable. We are all quite likely to do things when we are scared that we regret afterwards, and horses in parti-cular are by nature unpredictable and of a nervous disposition. Moreover everyone who rides should know the risks, and should understand their horse's temperament and limitations. However, the truly insubordinate horse really is dangerous, and the confirmed bolter is clever; he will undoubtedly have worked out a way of getting his tongue over the bit or of taking hold of it with his teeth. In fact if the bit is correctly fitted, it is all but impossible for him to take hold of it; moreover a flash or grakle noseband will stop him playing with the bit to a certain extent (though it should not be so tight that the mouth is clamped shut).

Certain horses seem more prone to bolting than others. Such a type is usually very nervous, and constantly tries to evade the bit whilst schooling by raising the head excessively. It may dash off in the school on the slightest excuse, and will generally take a few minutes to calm down, still fighting the contact. Riders who have experienced these problems at home would be well advised *not* to ride the horse out hacking, and should be very careful to avoid situations where the horse might be tempted to take off; these might include: going by oneself so no one can summon help, cantering at every spare moment on unknown territory, paying little attention to the horse, and riding with loose, relaxed reins. And if riding out is unavoidable, then the rider should take certain precautions: a stronger bit may be used (as long as the horse is used to working with it at home in the school; if he wears it for the first time when out hacking, the new feeling may make him even more anxious); also a running martingale could be used with a snaffle bit, as this may prevent the horse raising the head excessively – though condemned by some as tying the horse down, it may prove a life-saver if it gives the rider a little bit more control. Finally, riders should always keep to well frequented areas, and should maintain a sensible pace at all times.

So, what if all precautions have been taken, and the horse still bolts, or acts completely out of character and takes off suddenly and violently? What can riders do in these circumstances? They must act very fast, and should try to slow or turn the horse immediately. Constant sawing at its mouth will only serve to aggravate it even more, and leaning

A Fulmer snaffle: the long cheek-pieces should enable the rider to turn the horse more easily if it does take off.

back is also futile because it gives the horse more to pull against. So, as all subtleties are useless, the rider should push his hands up towards the horse's ears and then give several short, sharp pulls on the rein. Yes, it will hurt the horse, but it may provide the shock he needs to make him break out of his frenzy. The best option if there is sufficient space is to turn him sideways, making a circle which can then be decreased. Two hands may be needed to turn, though of course riders run the risk of turning the horse over. But providing they are not on hard tarmac, even this is preferable to being galloped onto a road and hit by a car.

If none of this works and the horse is still in a blind panic, riders should take whatever action they deem appropriate. Stories have been told of twisting or biting the horse's ear, or even grabbing the bit with the hands and pulling. However, when finally it is a matter of life or death, human life is more important and if you are approaching a busy road out of control, you should throw yourself off and leave the horse to it. This may seem callous, but it is surely preferable to being involved in a horrific car accident. Besides, the horse will be much quicker and nimbler without a rider, and so should be better able to dodge traffic and turn quickly.

Problems with lateral work

PROBLEM Why is it that some horses seem to have a mental block when it comes to lateral work? What is the best way to explain simply and clearly what is required?

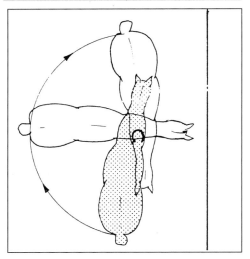

Turn on the forehand: a simple exercise which teaches the horse to move its quarters away from the rider's leg

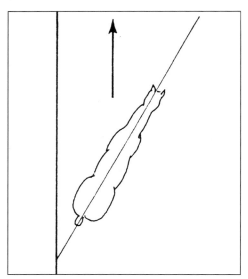

Leg-yielding: the horse moves forwards and sideways. If the movement is to the left he will be perfectly straight except for a slight bend to the right at the poll

SOLUTION Most of the problems which are associated with lateral work – that is, moving away from the leg – are actually caused by rider inexperience. Many are made nervous because they consider it to be 'dressage' and a separate entity from normal school movements; in fact lateral work is no more than a natural progression from general schooling. Indeed, all dressage work is still schooling, but just on a different level. All dressage riders practise 20m circles and transitions, and all started with the *basics* which every rider knows about. And lateral work starts in the stable: by standing next to the horse's side and pushing him across while saying 'over', the horse is learning to move away from pressure – this instruction is used in the stable all the time, and is a useful start to lateral work. When ridden, the horse should be going forwards sufficiently in his general schooling, and should be using his hocks for impulsion. The rider should have a good seat and light hands, and a thorough understanding of the aids. Riding with an experienced instructor is especially useful in the first stages of lateral work, particularly as he or she can get on and show both horse and rider what is required.

The first lesson is usually turn on the forehand, which simply teaches the horse to move its quarters away from the rider's leg: first, go forwards into a square halt, preferably facing the manège fence – let us assume that we wish to make a turn so that the quarters move over to the right. The left rein should ask for a slight inside bend, the right rein prevents the horse from walking forward. The right leg 'supports' the forehand and stays on, or slightly behind the girth. The left leg asks the quarters to move to the right, and should be behind the girth. The instructor can gently push the horse over for a stride or two and say 'over', so that it associates the action with the sound. Once the horse is parallel with the fence, it has made a quarter turn; if he turns so that he ends up facing the opposite way to his starting position he has made a half turn, and so on. The inside fore pivots on the same spot, and the inside hindleg crosses over the outside hindleg.

Leg-yielding involves moving forwards and sideways at the same time, and is most easily achieved when it is carried out on the quarter line of the school, about five metres from the fence along the long side. If the movement is to the left, the neck should have a slight bend or flexion to the right; the outside rein prevents too much forward motion. The outside leg will support the quarters and prevent swinging, positioned at the girth, and the inside leg will push the horse from its position just behind the girth. It will be more difficult for the instructor to assist as the horse is walking, but he or she will be able to advise on when to half halt or begin walking forwards again.

Most horses learn lateral work easily, providing they are supple and obedient. The rider should learn exactly what is required before attempting the movements – you might even try performing them as if you were the horse: yes, you might look foolish, but it will help you to understand exactly how the horse's body is expected to move.

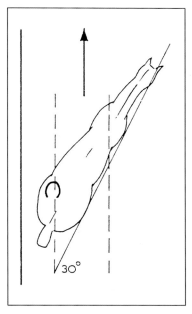

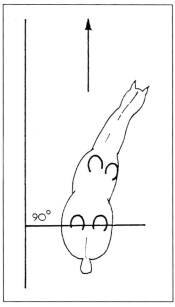

(left) Shoulder-in is a beneficial introduction to lateral work; (left) at an angle of 30° to the direction of movement, with little bend, and (right) with the hips positioned at right-angles to the track, and bend for a 15m circle. Shoulder-in improves suppleness and collection.

Suppling and obedience-improving exercises (below left to right): Travers, with the shoulders at 30° to the line of progress, and at 90°, with the hindquarters taken in; this can either be performed along the wall or on the centre line; renvers is the same exercise as travers, except that the forehand is brought in from the track (this diagram shows renvers from the half-pirouette); half-pass is a variation of travers, executed on the diagonal, and shown here from a 10m circle.

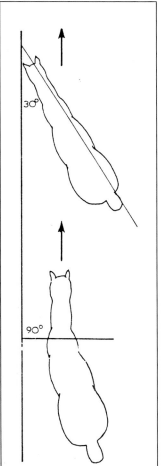

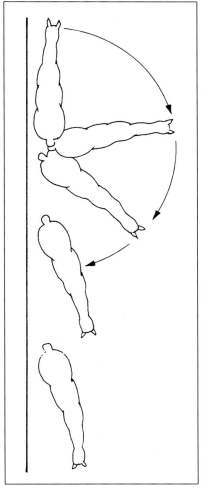

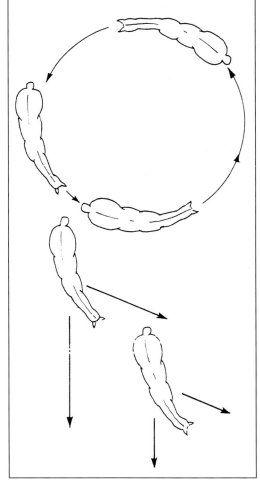

Preventing pulling

PROBLEM Horses pull for a variety of reasons, and will try to gain speed or move into a higher gait. This is of course unpleasant for the rider, who will feel as if he is not in control and therefore unable to school his horse consistently. Why does this happen, and how can the horse be taught to behave?

SOLUTION Some horses are badly trained, and may have been simply cantered around by an inexperienced rider who just enjoyed the thrill of fast riding. Perhaps the horse is running away from pain caused by sharp teeth or an injury or ill-fitting tack? He could have experienced pain previously, and now associates being ridden with discomfort. It is important to eliminate any physical reason, so the horse should first be examined by a veterinary surgeon and have his tack checked to ensure it fits correctly.

The rider may now assume that the horse is either very keen and anticipating some excitement, or is inexperienced, or disobedient, all of which require careful re-schooling. A common and natural mistake made by riders trying to slow a pulling horse is to pull back. Though this may be a last resort, it is not an effective schooling method as it will cause the horse to pull even more. He will probably lean on the contact, and fall further on to his forehand.

The treatment of this problem is correct riding: the rider must maintain a very firm leg, and ride the horse into a light contact. Easier said than done, but with persistence and patience it can be achieved. The rider should first block with the hand and maintain impulsion, then relax his rein contact a little so he is 'giving and taking'. When he gives with his rein the horse will take the contact, and he should sit quietly and praise the horse when he does well.

Try 'bridging the reins' with a hard-pulling horse; his own withers and neck will then take the force and weight of his pulling, and this is much less tiring for you, the rider.

It is important to school the horse kindly, using transitions to encourage him to use his hocks properly, and correct riding to establish a good rhythm and balanced stride. Lungeing may help, particularly as the rider can see if the horse moves differently without the interference of a rider. Changing the bit is an option, but need not necessarily mean moving to a stronger type; in fact the horse may be used to pulling against a harsh bit and will welcome a soft snaffle. If the horse works sensibly when schooled but pulls across country, it may be sensible to use a stronger bit in competition. It is a common misconception that a 'stronger' bit is cruel; it is not the bit that is strong, but the action it creates when controlled by a rider. Thus a heavy-handed rider may do much more damage using a jointed snaffle than an experienced rider with light hands using a curb bit. Consistent and varied schooling will prove beneficial in the long run, providing the rider is prepared to be patient!

Resisting the rein-back

SOLUTION The preparation for rein-back can begin while the horse is still young and in hand. Apply pressure to the chest and reins and he will soon realise that he is being asked to move back; moreover he will find it fairly easy to accomplish without a rider's weight. Before asking for the rein-back when ridden, the horse should fully understand and have accepted all the other ridden aids.

1   To ask for rein-back the rider's weight should be transferred slightly more onto the thighs, allowing the horse to bring up his back a little. The hands should then squeeze on the reins, applying a light pressure, while the legs are applied on the horse's side to guide him backwards in a straight line.

2   To stop the rein-back, the rider resumes a position more on the seat-bones, and the legs are closed more firmly onto the horse's sides.

3   If the horse is resisting, he will push his head up and his back down, making it physically very difficult for himself to step back. If he is made to go backwards in this sort of shape he will feel very uncomfortable, and this will not augur well for his next attempt; it will almost certainly have left him with a bad experience.

It is crucial that the horse does not associate the rein-back with something difficult: go back to work in hand if necessary, showing him that he can perform the movement comfortably after all. Once this has been accomplished, the process can be repeated with a rider just sitting on his back, but with an assistant asking for the movement from the ground. Progress to asking for rein-back through the correct aids, but introduce this gradually as the horse's confidence and response dictates.

It is important to recognise what constitutes a correct rein-back. In accurate rein-back the horse will keep a good outline, clearly lifting the off (right) foreleg and near (left) hindleg off the ground at the same time. A slight lowering of the hindquarters which ensures that the horse's weight stays off the forehand should also be detected.

PROBLEM Resisting against the pressure on the reins is a common problem during the execution of rein-back: either the horse refuses to move, half rears, or rushes back out of balance. What is the correct procedure for requesting rein-back? How do you judge if the horse is doing it correctly, and how should you teach the movement to a young horse? (See also Part 1, The Young Horse, page 44.)

When teaching a young horse to rein back for the first time, or if the more experienced horse is showing resistance, make sure you have an assistant on the ground who can encourage him backwards if needs be; if the rider has to pull or kick too strongly, the horse is bound to raise his head which will completely compromise the movement.

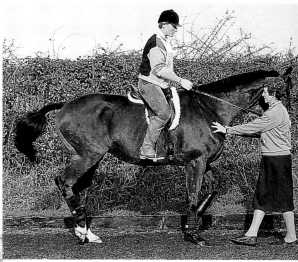

When teaching rein-back, in order to keep the movement straight, it helps to perform it along a school wall, or with some other straight barrier on one side. This provides a visual guide for the rider — although on no account should he be tempted actually to look backwards — and a psychological 'support' for the horse.

Traffic shy

PROBLEM Some horses are extremely traffic shy, whilst others seem unflappable and will walk past anything. Why is this so, and what can be done to re-educate the traffic-shy horse?

Most of our horses' fears and reservations can be traced back to their youth, and traffic shyness is no exception. The young horse whose field was close to a road experiences noise and vibrations from an early age, and learns to accept the sights and sound of traffic; and the horse which grew up on a busy farm with tractors in and out all the time and plenty of bustle will take it all in his stride! Therefore owners and riders should make every effort to accustom their horses to traffic as soon as possible, as later on in life this lack of experience could lead to all sorts of problems and trauma. Temperament is also a factor: some horses just deal with situations more rationally than others and see no reason to flee from a huge rattling object; others are scared to within an inch of their lives and will take avoiding action at first sight of anything that scares them.

SOLUTION It is best to begin the horse's traffic schooling at home, though help is needed in the process. In the safety of a schooling area or paddock, to help him learn to cope sensibly with unusual objects, someone can hold flapping plastic in front of the horse, or open an umbrella; he may be scared at first, but with repetition and perseverance he will almost certainly come to accept the objects; a soothing and encouraging voice is needed, together with firm riding so he learns to walk past them calmly. If it is possible to use some form of vehicle as part of the training, then all the better – perhaps a friendly tractor driver can be persuaded to park the vehicle in a field or driveway, where the horse can walk around it until he is accustomed to the sight. The process can then be repeated with the engine turned on, until he will walk past sensibly. This may seem impractical, but it is the perfect way to re-educate the traffic-shy horse: after all, if the only time he meets such vehicles is on the road, they are gone within minutes and may not be accommodating enough to stop and pull over. On familiar home ground the horse can spend as much time as he needs getting acquainted with the tractor, and can even be fed and stabled near to it. The same goes for horseboxes, cars and motorbikes: if the horse has some experience of them before venturing outside, he will accept other traffic more easily.

When taking the horse out onto the road, it is sensible to ride out with another more experienced or sensible animal on the outside, to box him in and give him the necessary confidence. Quiet country roads are of course the best place to start, as long as they are wide enough to ride two horses abreast safely. Once the inexperienced horse is used to oncoming cars from this position, he can be asked to walk slightly ahead of the other horse, until eventually he is a full length in front. This should be a gradual process, of course, and will take several sessions to accomplish. A similar approach may be taken with large vehicles on busier roads, keeping the inexperienced horse boxed in so he has a chance to gain confidence. He should be positioned so he can see the traffic, that is with his head turned towards

the road and not the hedge; moreover in this position the quarters will not swing out so easily.

If the horse is truly scared and will not walk past a vehicle, or is anxious because one is approaching from behind, riders are quite within their rights to ask it to stop by holding up their hand at shoulder level. And with the vehicle approaching from behind, it may be easier to turn round and walk past on the other side of the road, so the horse does not think he is being chased. Of course riders should always thank drivers, even if only with a nod of the head if their hands are full!

Most traffic-shy horses learn and improve with practice and repetition, though the process may take some time. Providing there is another horse alongside, and the rider is aware of the road and traffic conditions the whole time, the horse's fear can be conquered. There are usually, driveways or lay-bys to wait in if necessary, so read the road as the ride progresses – indeed, this practice is essential.

It is vital that both you and your horse are easily visible to motorists: they will then have plenty of time to slow down and overtake you. Reflective clothing is available from most saddlers, tack shops and agricultural suppliers.

Part 3:
JUMPING

The five stages of jumping

The jumping process can be broken down into five stages; identified thus, it is easier for the rider to concentrate on any one aspect whilst schooling or preparing to jump a course. Any of them may cause problems, and in order to evaluate and therefore try to solve these, it is important to understand fully exactly what is involved in the execution of each stage. So, what are the five stages of jumping, and how can the rider maintain positive and successful riding throughout them all? They are the approach, the take-off, suspension or flight, the landing and finally the getaway.

THE APPROACH

A correct approach is important, otherwise the horse may be off centre and at an angle which makes it difficult for him to jump. The rider must therefore make sure the horse is heading for the centre of the jump: he should be looking forwards and riding a straight line, ideally at right-angles to the fence for as many strides as possible, so the horse may establish his take-off point. In an indoor school or a small arena space may be limited, but the rider must allow as long a run-up to the fence as he can.

At this point the rider must have a deep seat: it should not be raised from the saddle in the jumping position. Like this he will be in a much better position to drive the horse forwards and to stay in the saddle if it shies or attempts refusal. The reins should be short enough for a good contact but not restricting, the weight down in the stirrups and the legs driving the horse forwards.

THE TAKE-OFF

It is at the take-off point that the accuracy of the horse's jump will be determined: too close, and he will be attempting to jump vertically, too far away and he will probably flatten and knock the fence. Either way is unseating and will cause discomfort for both rider and horse. The rider must try and 'see' the stride on his approach (see page 102), and place the horse at the jump so that it arrives at the best take-off point. Older and wiser horses may be best left alone, as they will probably alter their own stride if necessary and may resent interference; however, most young and inexperienced horses need assistance from their rider, and encouragement in the form of a firm squeeze with the leg.

At this point the rider may assume the jumping position, taking the weight forwards and off the horse's back, and allowing its neck to stretch by giving with the reins.

The horse should flow over the jump in a smooth bascule, and the degree of success with which he achieves this smoothness is directly related to the quality of his canter.

SUSPENSION OR FLIGHT

In flight the horse's body should make an arc shape over the fence – known as a bascule– with his neck stretched forwards and his legs tucked up neatly beneath him. Obviously this stage passes very quickly, but even so the rider must be thinking ahead to the next fence, and should prepare accordingly. It may be necessary for the horse to land on a certain leg after the fence, or to make a sharp turn in one direction – the rider should be sliding the appropriate leg back or squeezing with the rein while the horse is in the air, so that no time is wasted on landing.

THE LANDING

This stage also happens quickly, and the rider must try hard to allow the horse sort out his own balance and recovery without too much interference. He should sit up so his weight is no longer too far forwards, otherwise he may tip the horse too much onto the forehand and cause him to trip. The reins must be long enough so the horse can use his neck to balance, but not so long that there is no contact, thus allowing him to speed up too much or to stumble.

THE GETAWAY

This usually involves an approach to another fence, so the rider should be looking ahead and riding to the jump, whilst re-establishing the horse's rhythm, balance and speed. The horse may try to speed up, so the rider should sit deep in the saddle and check him with the rein to maintain control. On the other hand, if the fence is the last in a course, the rider may be riding hard to the finish, taking the shortest route and driving the horse forwards.

> *Of course when the rider is jumping he does not think in five stages, for there is no time: once he is reasonably competent he will be riding positively to the fence and looking out for the next one, the individual elements and jumping position coming naturally to him.*

Cross-country jumping

These five elements of jumping (see pp 86-7) apply at all levels, whether schooling a youngster in the field, or riding competitively against the clock. Each stage must also be considered when riding across country, even though the types of fences will be different and a different range of considerations must be taken into account, such as the changes in terrain and the more solid, broader fences.

Riders must keep a good approach in mind whatever the jump, though when riding across country they may have more chance of a straighter line. As the fences get higher the horse may need to jump out of his stride, and this may mean taking off a little further back. Fences approached downhill will also require a take-off point further away, as the horse will have to make undue effort if he gets too close. The take-off point is approximately one-and-a-half times the height of the fence; however, this is only a guideline from which riders may estimate the correct point according to their situation.

Obstacles with a higher level of difficulty such as water jumps and ditches will need careful placing; for instance, if the rider is jumping into water he will need to prepare for this by slowing the horse down on the approach. Jumping down a drop will require precision rather than speed, and jumping up a step needs a good deal of impulsion. Whatever the type of fence, the approach should be made at a steady but consistent pace, and the take-off point adapted to suit its size and shape. Most bold horses will get their riders out of trouble if they are unsure of the exact spot, so it is a good idea to ride an

The local hunter trial is an excellent way to introduce a horse to tackling fences at speed on his own.

exper-ienced horse over various fences to get an idea of what works. This practical knowledge may then be put to good use with an inexperienced horse, who may rely on his rider for guidance.

The landing over cross-country fences also needs careful consideration. Firstly, if the horse has approached at a faster pace he will land harder on the other side, so the rider must make sure his weight is not taken forwards so the horse strains his legs. Thus he should sit up and prepare immediately for the next fence, maintaining control lest the faster pace should accelerate. The style of jump may also be a deciding factor; for instance, when jumping down a drop the rider will need to slip the reins so the horse is allowed his head, and to take his weight backwards so the horse does not fall on his forehand. Jumping up a step or bank will require the rider to assist the horse by taking the weight forwards, so that momentum is not lost.

Basically riders must assess each fence according to its size and shape, and use the horse's stride and pace to their advantage. This comes with practice and an experienced eye.

At affiliated trials the fences will probably be more solidly built and will therefore look more imposing. In fact horses are often encouraged to jump more boldly if the fences look substantial.

The horse must learn to tackle all sorts of fence without hesitation – bullfinches, as here, drops and water should all be included in his education.

Backing off fences

PROBLEM   Some horses back off their fences when jumping, lacking both impulsion and enthusiasm. Why does this happen, and what can the rider do to prevent future occurrences?

In some cases backing off is not necessarily a bad thing, for example the experienced showjumper which slows down to assess the jump and re-adjust his stride. In fact, he will probably only back off for a split second, before propelling himself upwards with the quarters and taking off correctly.

CAUSE   When a horse backs off before his jump, he takes shorter and shorter strides on his approach until he has little impulsion left. He may get 'underneath the fence', when he is too close to take off properly, in which case he may refuse to jump at all, or if he does, he may knock it down; this may frighten him, and make him over-cautious the next time.

A horse may persistently back off either because he is by nature a very cautious jumper, or because he is just plain scared. This may be deep rooted, and could originate from a fall or bad knock-down, or because he has never been ridden positively. He will probably start the approach with plenty of impulsion, but as he nears the fence will put his ears back and take a good look at the jump. He will use his front end as a kind of brake so his quarters are no longer beneath him, and his impulsion will continue to dwindle until he reaches the fence, probably less than half a stride away from it. At this point if he is brave and willing he may attempt the jump, although he may not clear it unless he is very athletic. He is just as likely to refuse, unseating his rider who often ends up on his neck.

SOLUTIONS   **The willing but over-cautious horse**
If the horse is indeed willing but just over-cautious, careful schooling will probably help him to overcome this habit. It is important not to overface him, but to school over smaller fences, only raising them when he is comfortable and not backing off. The rider must be very positive, keeping a deep seat and really attacking the fence. This means strong aids, verbal encouragement and an almost aggressive attitude, because if the rider expects a refusal, how can the horse be expected to jump the fence? The rider may have had one too many falls, and on the approach to the fence is grabbing the mane or shortening the reins, which the horse takes as a pull on the rein to slow down. A placing pole one stride away from the fence may help the horse to establish his rhythm, and give him the extra confidence he needs.

The unwilling and scared horse
This sort of horse is unlikely to make a really good jumper – he may do well at local level, but when the fences get higher he needs complete trust in his rider and a bold, scopey jump if he is to succeed. The rider must therefore be sure the horse is not scared of him, and that it is responsive to the aids and voice; this may be achieved by careful lungeing and schooling. Nor must the horse ever be allowed to get bored of jumping, so a good mix of jumping and flatwork should be included in his schooling programme.

If the horse is genuinely scared, the rider must take him back to basics and school him over grids and a variety of low fences. Perhaps the course at a competition was too big for him and scared him, and he may need to regain his confidence over lower fences. It is much better for the horse to jump a lower fence with style and confidence, than to scramble over a large fence and be scared.

As before, the rider must be firm and positive in his riding, maintaining a deep seat on the approach to a fence so he may drive the horse forwards. Again, a pole placed one stride in front of the jump may help to increase the horse's confidence and rhythm. The rider may need to use the whip at the horse's shoulder if he feels him backing off (using it behind the leg will involve a change of contact on the reins, resulting in a confused horse). Of course the horse must not fear the whip, but he should know it is there and respond accordingly; a sharp tap may be all the encouragement he needs to wake him up and provide a surge of speed.

An experienced rider will generally be only too well aware if he has overfaced his horse, and he should always be careful to avoid doing so because it can take a long time and a great deal of schooling to rebuild its trust and restore its confidence.

Refusing

PROBLEM Why do some horses refuse when asked to jump, and how can the problem be prevented in the future?

CAUSE All horses refuse fences at some stage in their jumping life, stopping suddenly and often with so much force that they either fall into the fence themselves, or dislodge their rider, a situation which is dangerous for all concerned. The reasons for refusing are varied, and in fact sometimes there may not appear to be a reason at all – we all know the nature of horses:

◆ The most basic reason for a horse persistently stopping is fear, and this is nearly always the case in a young horse which is still learning. He may spook at a particularly strange-looking fence, perhaps one that is brightly coloured or of a different shape. In the first instance the refusal is only to be expected, though the rider must make every effort to encourage the horse over the jump at his first attempt, lest refusing becomes a habit.

◆ An error may have occurred in the rider's approach, and perhaps the horse has ended up too close to the fence, or has rushed into the jump and panicked at the last moment. The approach itself may not have been straight, or the horse may not have had enough time to prepare for the jump and may have run out. This is why it is so important that the approach is carefully thought out, and the rider should slow the pace down if necessary, or turn a circle in order to ride at the fence straight and at a sensible speed.

The rider himself must always compensate for his horse's lack of confidence by riding purposefully and firmly: if he is nervous or unsure it will be transmitted to the horse. It is best to maintain a deep seat until he is sure the horse will take off, because if he leans forwards or alters the contact the horse may lose confidence and momentum, and drop into the fence.

Basic schooling exercises to improve the horse's balance and obedience, and so help the rider to keep him between hand and leg, include lengthening and shortening the stride (top right); trotting poles (centre right); and jumping through an inverted 'V' of poles (right and far right).

- The horse may be nervous of jumping because of the conditions: slippery or boggy ground is disconcerting and hazardous, and a high wind or intense cold may put him in a bad mood, making him unco-operative.
- The day-to-day relationship between horse and rider may be partly to blame for a refusal: the horse may be disobedient and undisciplined, the rider may be lacking in perseverance, or the will or ability to ride firmly. And if the horse gets his own way in his flatwork, he will undoubtedly do so in his jumping, too.

SOLUTION

In order to prevent a refusal, the rider must be very firm and should really drive the horse forwards. On the approach to a fence, the line must be kept straight, and the pace and rhythm consistent. The horse must be listening to the rider and not fighting the contact – this would mean he was not concentrating, and it might induce a refusal. The hocks should be propelling the horse forwards, and impulsion must be maintained. As soon as the rider does not contain the impulsion between leg and hand, the horse will feel that the rider has given up and will immediately lose confidence. Of course, if none of this is happening, the rider cannot expect the horse to jump correctly, and must return to the basics and improve the horse's flatwork first.

Rushing fences

PROBLEM Some horses increase their speed on approach to a fence, rushing and consequently losing their rhythm. What causes them to do this, and how can it be prevented in future?

CAUSE Rushing into fences is quite a common problem, and one seen frequently at shows when a round or a jump-off is timed. Typically, the horse may begin with a nice established rhythm, but as he gets nearer to the fence he speeds up, resulting in a very nasty refusal or an untidy jump.

There are several causes of this problem, most rider-induced. The excited horse is one exception, as he may simply be highly strung and enjoying his jumping. However, no matter how excitable he is, the fact that he is allowed to get away with rushing means that he is either badly schooled or disobedient. 'He's just excited' is a likely excuse from a rider who thrives on speed and excitement himself. A stronger bit may be the answer in this case, if only on a short-term basis until the horse has learned to respect his rider's wishes.

◆ A common cause is pain somewhere in the horse's body, most likely the back or the mouth. An existing back pain will be greatly exacerbated by the back muscles stretching during jumping, and a rider who jabs with the reins or uses them to balance himself will greatly aggravate the horse. Any physical pain must be eliminated before the rider can assume that the rushing is a schooling problem.

◆ Many horses are just not terribly bold when it comes to jumping, and may quite simply be scared; this will cause some to back off, whilst others rush at the jump to get it over with. Some horses are willing, but not bold enough, and these may rush their approach and still jump the fence – though one might imagine it is with their eyes shut and hoping for the best! These horses start off with every intention of jumping, but at the last instant their nerve fails and they suddenly refuse or crash into the jump. Unfortunately their rider may have been convinced they would take off, and have assumed the jumping position – only to be unseated.

Lungeing or loose jumping the horse over a jump without the rider may well pinpoint the cause. For instance, if the horse is tense and short in the neck when ridden, but is relaxed and stretches his neck when lunged, then rider intervention is almost certainly causing pain.

SOLUTION With young horses which rush it is generally not too late to re-school them; they may have been overfaced by an over-enthusiastic trainer, and just need to return to basics for a while. In an older horse the problem will be more deeply established, and he may never be reliable in competition. He too must be taken back a stage, and schooled over grids and small jumps to help him regain his confidence. In this case a stronger bit is probably not the answer, since the horse needs to learn to trust his rider and also to believe in his own ability. A grid of one-stride and bounce fences should be set up, and the horse kept at a slow and steady pace throughout. The approach should be made in trot, and every effort taken to encourage and praise the horse. Placing poles in front of single jumps may help him maintain a better rhythm. The rider must be sure to help him as much as possible, keeping the approach steady and the pace slow, and giving the aids to take off when necessary.

Aversion to coloured poles

CAUSE When the young horse learns to jump, his initial schooling will be the basis for all future work. Thus many jumping problems may be traced back to this first stage – though whether or not they can be put right will depend on how seriously ingrained they are. It is likely that the horse which prefers rustic poles did all his initial jumping over them, and was never given the chance to become accustomed to brightly coloured equipment in his formative years.

The horse's temperament may influence his ability to get used to new poles, and if he is naturally spooky and nervous he may be unwilling to compromise for a while. Unfortunately there is no quick solution, and riders will need to persevere before the horse improves.

SOLUTION The first step is to accustom the horse to the new equipment in his everyday life: to this end, lay out coloured poles at random in the schooling area so he may walk over them as he is being worked. They need not be laid out in specific jumping distances, just placed here and there in the school so the horse can continue his normal schooling programme over them. If he is particularly scared or silly he may refuse even to go near them, in which case only one or two poles should be put down, with an assistant on hand to lead him over them. The rider must drive him forwards and keep a firm seat, guiding him with the reins (a few inches away from the neck if necessary) and praising him when he co-operates.

If the horse walks over rustic poles with no problem, he will eventually walk over the coloured ones, although his rider will need to instil plenty of confidence in him first. Once one pole has been accomplished the horse can be asked to walk over several more in the school, in time trotting over them, too.

Once the horse has got used to walking and trotting over the poles he can start to canter over them; they should be laid out so they are distance-related, starting with just one and then adding more at one canter stride apart. Should the horse be scared and shy away from the poles he should be allowed to trot or walk over them until he shows no alarm or resistance. Three poles may be laid down at the distance of a one-stride double fence, and five poles at the distance of a three-stride double, or a treble fence. Once the horse is used to this exercise the distances may be left as they are and jumps added.

Next, the jumps may be built up gradually into a grid (see page 108), keeping the fences very low and several strides apart. This exercise may be repeated a few times a week, also walking the horse over the ground poles throughout his schooling sessions. He might be asked to pop over a coloured fence at the end of his flatwork, too. Thus he is bound to be getting used to the poles all the time, and accepting them as part of his everyday life.

PROBLEM Some horses are unwilling to jump coloured poles, and seem to be more at ease over rustic or plain jumps. What causes this aversion, and how can the horse be re-educated?

A good way to introduce a horse to brightly coloured fillers is to use the sort that come in two parts; to begin with these can be placed one on each side of the fence, then at each successive jump they can be drawn further into the middle until they meet – and the horse should sail over with no fuss!

A useful exercise is to form a square of coloured poles so that once the horse has walked over one, he is surrounded by them. He should then be made to halt and stand still for a few minutes, perhaps being given some food so he associates the poles with something pleasant. It may also help to lead him over the poles on his way to the field every day, and to feed him inside the square every meal-time.

Trotting pole excitement

PROBLEM Many horses become excitable, presented with a line of trotting poles or a grid of small jumps, and will often leap about, or jump up and down on the spot instead of going calmly forwards over the obstacles. When pushed, they will then plunge forwards, perhaps trying to jump two or more poles at a time. Why is this, and how can a horse be calmed down during jump training?

CAUSE This problem often has its roots in poor initial schooling, usually because the horse was either rushed or frightened. Certainly some horses do have an excitable temperament, but this is all the more reason for taking time with them when they are young. In order to solve the problem the horse needs to be taught that jumping is still work, and that he must therefore behave in a calm and mannerly way.

SOLUTION

1   Before the horse is schooled he should be taken out for a hack so he can burn up any excess energy – although he should not be exercised to the point where he is tired.

2   Then he should be taken into the school where poles have been put down at random on the ground. He should be walked around the school, and when he reaches a pole the rider should not change position, or do anything other than just keep the aids for walking calmly forwards. The idea is for the horse just to step over each pole as and when he encounters it, rather than being made to approach them on purpose. This also prevents the rider 'setting the horse up' for the pole, which is guaranteed to alert him to something 'exciting'.

3   Once he will walk calmly and happily over the poles around the school, he can then be moved into trot, employing the same tactics. On no account should the horse be 'collected' for the poles, and if he tries to rush, the rider should check him and simply keep the aids constant and gentle. The more the horse is allowed to 'potter' around the poles in this way, the less they will hold any excitement for him.

4   Once this has been accomplished, the poles can then be set out in a line; but rather than using closely placed poles as is usual – which can lead the horse to attempt to jump them – they should be spaced about 3^1/$_2$m (12ft) apart. Not only will this discourage the horse from jumping them, it will also provide an ideal schooling aid for different exercises.

5   The aim is to establish a consistent and unhurried rhythm, whatever the activity. To do this the horse needs to be brought between hand and leg, using his hindquarters more effectively and therefore becoming more supple. All the work is done at a walk until the horse seems quite settled. The following exercises may be helpful; they can be performed in any order:

◆ Walk over a line of poles, but circle the horse away at various points down the line, either left or right (diagram 1).

◆ Walk over the poles, and at various points stop and pat the horse before walking on over the remaining poles.

◆ Walk through the line of poles as if performing a serpentine (diagram 2).

◆ Walk over the first two poles, circle away to the right, walk back down the line then circle away to the left after the fourth pole (diagram 3).

◆ Walk over the whole line of poles in one go.

6   The idea is to prevent the horse anticipating the next move and so acting on what he *thinks* the rider wants, rather than on the aids the rider has actually given. Once he is settled in walk, the exercises can be repeated in trot. Alternate with walk exercises so that he does not become excited. If he does he should be taken back to walk and allowed to relax mentally before moving on again.

7   Once the horse is totally relaxed with pole work, a cross-pole can be put up at the end of the line, but so low that he can still just step over it; no extra effort on the rider's part should have to be made in order to negotiate it – the horse should simply be allowed to step over it. The circling exercises can be continued in order to prevent him anticipating. Once settled, the cross-pole can be raised, but only gradually in order to keep the horse settled. How well he progresses will depend quite a lot on how calm and consistent the rider can be.

8   When he copes calmly with the exercise so far, another fence can be added 6–7m (21–24ft) after the first to form a combination (note that the distance must be adapted to suit the length of the individual horse's stride).

These exercises will take time, but the longer the horse is given at this stage the less likely it is that he will revert to his old habit of 'rushing' when he starts jumping again.

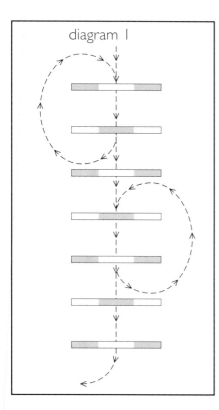

diagram 1

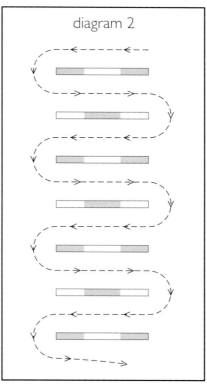

diagram 2

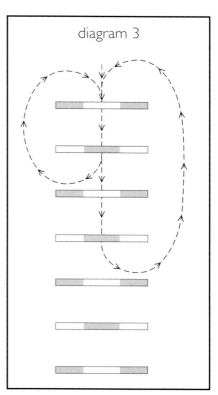

diagram 3

Lungeing and loose schooling over jumps

PROBLEM Lungeing is a useful part of the schooling process and can help to solve many jumping-related problems. Lungeing a horse over jumps without a rider allows him to gain his own balance and sort out his own stride without the hindrance of extra weight.

This horse has taken off very close indeed to the fence, yet he is still clearing it: with a rider he might have refused, but lungeing gives him the confidence to sort things out for himself and to keep going.

HOW TO DO IT Initially he should be lunged over poles, three being a good number: too many poles will confuse him, and too few will not be worthwhile. The poles should be placed on a circle, with the distance between them wider at their outer end; the horse will then be able to walk on the inside and trot on the outside of the circle without the need for moving the poles.

At first the lunge work should be kept in walk and trot; the horse should be lunged on both reins until he is happy with the poles, and is picking up his feet nicely. Next the middle pole may be raised a few inches at the outside; this is to encourage the horse to look at what he is doing, and to lift up his feet better whilst maintaining an unhurried rhythm. Next the first and third poles can be raised at the inside, and the exercise repeated on both reins.

When a jump is introduced, it is often better not to use ground poles so as not to confuse the horse. A small cross-pole should be set up, with low wings so the lunge-line does not get entangled; placing the poles on oil drums or something of a similar size will be quite adequate. The horse should be brought round on a wide circle, so he has time to see the jump and take a straight approach to its centre. If the circle is too tight the fence will be upon him before he knows it, and he is quite likely to refuse. However, there should be no reason for this: he should simply trot into the cross-pole and pop over it as if it were a raised pole. If he does refuse, he should be taken round on the circle once more, and asked to approach the fence calmly with verbal encouragement from the handler. A small flick with the lunge whip should motivate him if necessary.

The horse may well go into canter after the jump, but the handler should not worry about this, or about correct strides or the correct leading leg – he should just continue the circle away from the jump and bring the horse down to trot when he can, making sure the horse has re-balanced himself before re-approaching. The horse will learn to find his own stride in this way, providing his approach is straight and unhurried. At a later date the same exercise may be tried with a rider, though he must be sure to go with the horse and not interfere with his rhythm.

PROBLEM Many horses start to misbehave when jumping because they are badly ridden. Loose schooling over jumps can help in evaluating how much the horse has been spoilt, and can also help to re-educate him. So, what exactly does it involve, and how is it beneficial to the horse?

PURPOSE Loose schooling is exactly what it says: the horse is loose in the schooling area and is asked to jump a number of jumps – usually in a lane – with no physical intervention from a rider or handler. There are good and bad points to this method of schooling, and how successful it is depends very much on the facilities available and the expertise of the handler.

Loose schooling is not recommended for anyone who has not seen how it is done, and does not fully appreciate what is required. Such a person should find out about it first by watching others, and then by practising with an experienced horse and trainer. The aim is for the horse to jump quite on his own so he may find his own stride and his own rhythm, and is neither rushed nor hurried by the handler or rider. Conducted successfully, it should improve communication between horse and rider, and will test the horse's obedience. However, too many inexperienced handlers unfortunately run around the schooling area flapping and shrieking at the horse, which is then expected to jump a solitary fence in unhurried style.

THE LANE

There is little point in attempting to loose school without some sort of jumping lane, as the horse may run out and become over-excited or anxious. A jumping lane is the width of an average jump – about 8–10ft (3m) – generally on an oval track in an area of about 200ft (60m) square. A permanent lane is expensive to build, but is most beneficial to training yards which have a large turnover of horses; however, such yards will usually hire out this facility for a small fee. The jumps are placed across the lane so the horse cannot run out, though they should not be fixed to the sides.

Trainers without a permanent lane may construct a temporary one in the enclosed space of a manège or school by setting up a 'fence' of poles balanced on oildrums or Blox parallel to the manège fence on one long side. This improvised lane can prove just as useful if safely constructed. The poles should be set out in a grid and the strides measured, perhaps starting at one or two canter strides apart; bounce strides may then be added to encourage the horse to adapt his own stride. The number of fences will depend on the space available in the manège, though handlers must make sure there is sufficient approach and get-away space before and after the fences.

HOW TO DO IT

Before entering the jumping lane, the horse should be warmed up and quite supple. He should be taken into the lane and then sent up the middle, the trainer allowing him quite a long run up to his first fence. The trainer should encourage him to jump verbally, using the same commands as if he were lungeing. Additional handlers should be positioned round the lane two or three metres before each jump, to help send the horse forwards and provide encouragement. There are usually four to six jumps round a lane, and knocked poles should be quickly replaced before the horse comes round again. The handler should carry a schooling whip to help drive the horse forwards once more should he stop or refuse. The horse will tire quickly, so sessions should be kept relatively short, allowing him to jump on both reins, and giving him plenty of time to wind down and cool off afterwards.

As previously mentioned, it is imperative that a loose schooling session is set up and conducted properly, so the horse is not taught to dash about and jump wildly.

Most horses thoroughly enjoy being loose-schooled: this one is throwing a huge jump in good style even over the little cross-pole!

Learning to adapt the stride

PROBLEM Many horses encounter difficulty when their rider asks them to lengthen or shorten their stride. However, as both horse and rider progress with their jumping, it becomes increasingly important that the horse can adapt its stride to suit the course. How can riders teach their horses to shorten or lengthen on request?

SOLUTION Those riders who can 'see a stride' when they are on their horse (see page 102) may have noticed that he finds certain combination fences and grids difficult. In competition courses the fences are not always positioned at a set distance in relation to each other, as horses of different sizes and with varying strides will be competing, so it is helpful if the rider knows when and how he must alter his horse's stride to cope with the distances set.

Riders should know what kind of stride their horse has: is it long and scopey, or short and compact? For showjumping, a short compact stride is probably more useful, particularly where corners and sharp turns are concerned. Riders should also work out how many of their own strides relate to that of their horse, so that when they walk a course or set up a grid they will know where they will have to adapt their horse's stride. To work this out it is imperative to have an assistant present, as it is highly impractical for the rider to keep dismounting if poles are dislodged.

First, the poles should be laid out for approximately five canter strides, though of course the distance may depend on facilities and space – it may have to be set for three canter strides. They should be set up on a flat piece of ground, with plenty of room and initially on a straight line. Canter poles one stride apart may also be used for walking and trotting: there should be three walk steps, two trot steps and one canter stride in between each pole These should be adapted

A ground pole placed in front of a jump will help both horse and rider judge exactly where to take off.

until they suit the horse's normal stride, and the rider may warm up over them in walk, trot and canter.

The next exercise is to practise shortening and lengthening the stride over this set distance. The inner poles should be removed so there are just two, one at each end. Again the horse should walk, trot and canter over them, at his usual speed and with his 'normal' stride; without the poles to guide him, he may try to speed up, and the rider should be aware of this and keep the speed and impulsion consistent.

The next step is to canter over the poles, but checking the pace a little so as to shorten the horse's stride in order to fit six strides between the poles. The rider should keep a check on the outside rein and sit deep in the saddle, so the horse engages his hocks and his outline becomes shorter and more compact. Striking off to canter over the first pole may help if the horse finds this difficult. Once the horse has accomplished the exercise it should be repeated a few times, before lengthening and going back to the original five strides.

The next step is to practise lengthening the stride between the poles, so the horse covers the same distance in four strides. The rider will need to drive forwards more and ask for much more impulsion, though taking care not to let the horse rush or even gallop off out of control. It may be necessary for the assistant to bring the poles in a little if this part is too difficult, only moving them back to their original position as the horse progresses.

Once the horse can manage the complete exercise – which may well take several schooling sessions to achieve properly – small jumps may be placed where the poles were, gradually raised as horse and rider become more proficient. Eventually the exercise may be attempted on a large circle, though it must be carried out with plenty of room and only using as many strides as the horse can manage comfortably.

Seeing a stride

PROBLEM Many riders have a problem in 'seeing a stride' for a fence. A bold horse will take control and jump off whatever stride suits him, long or short. Should a horse be allowed to jump off his own natural stride, or should the rider make every effort to learn to 'see a stride'?

What is important is to know how the distance set relates to the individual horse: thus eight of your strides between two fences may represent quite a short one stride for a scopey Thoroughbred, but a very long stride for a dumpy, short-legged cob. Thus when the rider jumps the horse over the double, he will know whether or not his horse needs to lengthen to manage the one stride in between the fences, or to shorten up and take a smaller stride. The only way to accomplish this is with practice, gradually learning to see the stride, and getting to know the horse and how he likes to jump.

It is not a good idea for the horse to take control when jumping because he may jump less efficiently, perhaps flattening over a fence rather than using himself athletically, as is desired. However, a horse will only usually take control because he realises the rider is not giving him any commands. This can lead to a lack of confidence, and worse, a horse that stops listening to his rider. 'Seeing a stride' is not some elusive quality that only top riders can achieve: it comes through practice, and practice alone, and every rider can learn the skill.

'Seeing a stride' is being able to tell how many strides the horse will take between fences, and how many he will take on the approach to a fence in order to arrive at the optimum take-off point. It is about judging distance, and estimating the number of strides the horse will take to cover that distance.

SOLUTION A rider should start by watching the horse working, preferably being schooled by someone else and not by lungeing it himself, as he may not be concentrating if he is watching the ground. He should watch the horse's canter rhythm, counting 'one two three, one two three' as its feet hit the ground. Obviously it helps if the horse has a good rhythm, as an uneven pace will be difficult to follow. The rider should also be able to count the rhythm when he is in the saddle, feeling the stride with his seat and counting the beats out loud.

◆ The next step is for the rider to watch the horse jumping, counting the canter strides as he approaches a fence – he could even try saying 'one two three, jump' out loud as the horse approaches, so he recognises the number of strides the horse takes over a certain distance before the jump. He should then try this as he is riding, counting the last three strides into the jump. It does not matter if initially he gets them wrong, and estimates a greater or lesser number of strides than the horse actually takes – he will learn by repetition, and will get it right eventually.

◆ Next the rider should pace out a distance known to be a certain number of horse strides – for instance, if the horse has just been jumping a double set at one stride in between the jumps, the rider should walk the distance himself so he can equate his strides to that of his horse. Normally one assumes four of one's own strides for every one of a horse's; thus if the distance between the double is eight human strides, then you would divide the eight strides by four, as that is the number of strides you equate for every one of the horse's. Next you would take away one from the sum, as the horse will take off half a stride before the fence, and land half a stride away. Therefore, eight divided by four is two, and two minus one is one – and that is the number of strides the horse will need in between the fences. It sounds very complicated, but in practice it is not at all difficult to grasp.

1 First, the rider should be sure that he or she has control of the horse's stride, and can shorten or lengthen it on command. This can be achieved by basic schooling, through the use of upward and downward transitions and half-halts.

2 Poles can then be laid on the ground, which the rider imagines are jumps. He or she approaches in canter and practises lengthening or shortening the horse's stride in order to reach the pole at the optimum point of take-off. The rider must be positive, and insist that the horse listens and obeys the aids to alter the stride length.

3 A pole can then be put on the ground 2.75 or 3m (9 or 10ft) in front of a jump; the rider approaches the pole as before in a good, steady rhythm, but then kicks on over the fence. This will help to ensure the horse takes off at the desired time, offering the rider the correct 'feel'. The more this is practised, the easier seeing a stride becomes. However, the rider should not learn to rely on the 'placing' pole, which should be removed as soon as possible, so that she can practise without.

A placing pole positioned 2.75 or 3m (9 or 10ft) from the jump will ensure that the horse takes off at the right time

No respect for small fences

PROBLEM   Some horses seem not to respect smaller fences, rushing and consequently flattening over them. How can the horse with this problem be taught to jump correctly over all fences?

CAUSE   Although this situation seems to be the fault of the horse, in fact the rider could well be causing the problem by bad riding, albeit unwittingly. Also, the horse should have learnt to respect all fences by being schooled over grids of varying sizes, not just over large fences. So, what causes this lack of respect?

◆   The horse may love his jumping so much that he sees little point in making much effort over jumps he obviously considers too small for his ability. There are such horses about, and they have quite an attitude problem.

◆   The horse may be of an excitable nature, and although larger fences may slow him down and oblige him to concentrate, he perhaps cannot help himself rushing through the smaller, easier jumps in a frenzy.

◆   Some competition-minded riders seem to have a mental block when it comes to schooling, and inadvertently spoil their horses when in an effort to win the prizes in a showjumping class, they abandon precision and style in favour of speed. And when the jump is less difficult, the horse goes even faster.

SOLUTIONS   When a horse rushes over a fence he flattens, losing the rounded shape, or 'bascule', and consequently jumping with a hollow back; he may well take off early, too, so he does not get close enough to the fence, often landing awkwardly and with little balance. To prevent this, and to help him keep a good shape, it is important for any horse which jumps regularly to continue throughout his training with basic exercises, such as walking on the approach to a fence, and jumping grids and bounces. Many riders do not do this.

◆   To help the horse maintain a good bascule over a fence the rider must take care to give with the hands when he takes off – although he should not throw the contact away altogether, or the horse will tip onto his forehand. The rider must also be careful to maintain a deep seat and keep the hands low, so the horse does not fight the contact and raise his head. The key words are balance, rhythm and control, the rider keeping these in mind as he approaches the fence.

◆   It is important to practise over small fences at home, and not just the sort that will be encountered at a show. A grid of bounce fences at a canter stride apart (approximately 9ft/2.7m) will make the horse concentrate, as he will have great difficulty in flattening over these. The closer the fences are together, the more the horse will have to work and look at what he is doing. A line of five fences is usually adequate, though more may be added; be careful not to overdo things, however, as this exercise is demanding work for any horse.

◆ Frequent transitions correctly executed will also oblige the horse to use his hocks, thereby encouraging a more compact, rounded shape. It is often helpful to intersperse jumping with flatwork, so the horse is kept on his toes and does not anticipate what is coming next. This should also have a calming effect, particularly if the pace is slowed down and school movements in walk are carried out after gridwork.

Horses are easily scared, and it doesn't take much to put them off their work and effectively take a step backwards in their schooling programme. If a horse is naturally cautious the rider's job is in some ways made easier because the question of testing his courage, and thus risking overfacing him, does not arise. However, if the horse is intelligent, willing, and learns very quickly, it may be extremely tempting to rush his progress. For example, at a show recently a girl was jumping a four-year-old, which had in fact only been broken to saddle for a month. He was clearing the fences beautifully, if a little too fast, and was placed in his class. Of course the girl was delighted – but how tempting would it be to try him over increasingly bigger courses until his confidence suddenly gave out? A 'progressive training' means that a horse builds steadily on experience and confidence, so that he copes sensibly with mistakes, and doesn't panic or lose courage. After all, there is no rush, and the safest policy is to let the horse progress at his own speed.

Overfacing a horse

PROBLEM It is important when schooling not to overface the horse. How do riders know when to stop raising the height of a jump so as not to spoil previous good work?

SOLUTION With this in mind it is important while schooling to set a realistic goal for the session, and to try to achieve it. On some days this may mean finishing in half the usual time, on others it may take longer than was anticipated; the important thing is to finish on a good note. Horses learn by simple repetition, and cramming too much into one session may confuse and dishearten them. After all, they are generally willing to please, and will understand what you are trying to teach them quite easily if lessons are presented slowly and consistently.

As far as jumping is concerned, it is very important to keep everything within the horse's capabilities, and for most of the time well below this mark. Once the horse is more experienced and wiser his courage may be tested more fully – but until that time the fences must be kept at a sensible height, and should be raised and made more difficult only progressively. Overfacing is relative to what exercise the horse is doing; thus he may be happily jumping a 2ft (60cm) grid, until the rider puts up a 4ft (1.2m) upright at the end. The horse will probably refuse even though he is capable of jumping the fence – but he would most likely jump it quite happily on another day if it was raised gradually.

(opposite)
(a) Trotting the horse up to make sure he isn't lame.
(b) The physiotherapist treating the horse's back in case of possible strain.
(c) Basic gridwork will help to restore lost confidence.

So, how do riders know what their horse can reasonably manage? It depends entirely on the individual horse: who would ever have imagined that Marion Coakes, a young girl, and Stroller, a 14.2hh pony, would be placed at the Olympic Games? Of course few, if any ponies are capable of jumping such a demanding course – but Stroller's rider knew instinctively his abilities and limitations. The rider of any horse must be able to recognise immediately when he is unhappy or uncomfortable with what is asked of him, and when he is ready and able. This comes down to intuition and experience, and also knowing the horse. However, generally speaking, if the horse is happy jumping a certain height and jumps with inches to spare, the fence may be raised a notch. In one schooling session it would be unwise to raise the fence any more, but would be better to concentrate instead on the style and accuracy of the existing jump; the fence may be raised another notch on another day, as long as the horse is not showing signs of caution or discomfort.

The same goes for the type of jump as well as the height, as spreads, brushes and water jumps may also overface the horse if they are not introduced gradually. In short, the rider must just use his common sense, and if he is in any doubt as to how he should proceed, he should follow the advice of an experienced friend or instructor.

Dragging the hindlegs when jumping

PROBLEM It is important that the horse picks up his feet whilst jumping so he does not catch the poles and scare or hurt himself, or incur penalties in a showjumping competition. So, why do some horses drag their hindlegs when they are jumping, and how can they be re-educated?

CAUSE It is not in a horse's nature to drag his feet, as horses are normally quick and nimble creatures with powerful hindquarters. So, what causes this problem? When a young horse is being taught to jump he may well be a little careless, perhaps tripping over a pole or trailing a leg through lack of experience and insufficient muscle development. In the older horse the problem may arise because he wasn't made to pick his feet up and be careful when young, and has just developed a lazy habit.

Or the horse may be suffering discomfort or pain somewhere in his back – a typical sign of back pain is to dip the loins when pressure is put on the sore point. Observing the horse from the ground may determine what is causing the pain; for instance, the saddle may be slipping forwards or backwards, or the rider may be leaning back and unbalancing the horse, causing strain.

SOLUTIONS

◆   The horse's saddle should be checked for a correct fit by a saddler; if the fit is good, but the saddle is still slipping, a breastplate or crupper may be used to stop it slipping backwards or forwards

Riders may choose to have an assistant on the ground with a lunge or schooling whip, which may be flicked near the horse's hindquarters as he jumps. However, care must be taken not to entangle the end of the whip with the horse's legs – the whip should be more of a threat than an actual punishment.

respectively – these do not serve to correct an ill-fitting saddle, but should maintain its position throughout movement if the horse's conformation is at fault and causing the problem.

◆ Have the horse examined by a veterinary surgeon or physiotherapist, as any physical discomfort or ailment will not just disappear without examination or treatment. The vertebrae just behind the saddle often constitute a problem area where back pain is concerned, because the saddle may be lifting up and down as the horse jumps. Alternatively, the rider may be bumping down on the horse's back and causing bruising.

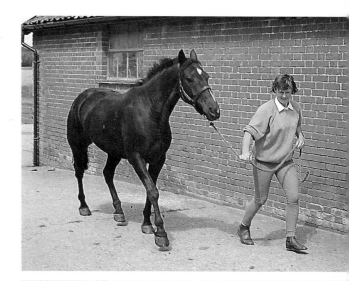

◆ Corrective schooling is necessary to teach the horse to pick up his feet; it is advisable to take the horse back to basic schooling work and use ground poles. These should be laid out in a grid or circle, so he learns to pick his feet up as he is walking. Competing should be curtailed until the horse improves, as the excitement of a show may cause him to lose concentration and drag his feet again.

◆ Further exercises with ground poles include the following: place the poles in a straight line, one canter stride apart (approximately 9ft/2.7m, or three human strides); on a circle they can be fanned, so the outside may be used for trot (4ft 6in/1.3m apart, or one-and-a-half human strides) and the inside for walk (3ft/90cm, or one human stride). Keep the exercise in walk to start with, riding on both reins and maintaining impulsion all the way.

Next the poles may be raised at one end, so that one pole is raised a few inches on the inside, the next is raised on the outside, the next on the inside again, and so on. Tyres or bricks provide a good height to begin with. Then the poles can be raised at both ends, the horse still walking over them; like this he will have to make a decided effort as he steps over them.

Once this is accomplished, a course of bounce fences may be laid out, so the landing point for each fence is also the take-off point for the next. This is a canter exercise, so the poles should be approximately 9ft apart – though the distance will have to be measured to suit the horse's stride. (Note that trotting over raised poles and this bounce canter exercise are very demanding, so riders must be careful not to go on for too long.)

◆ General suppling exercises on the lunge and in the school should also help to improve the problem, in time. Transitions will encourage the horse to bring his hocks underneath him; the rider should use firm leg aids and a deep seat.

Gridwork

PROBLEM

What exactly is a 'grid', and how useful is gridwork in the schooling of horses? Is a grid difficult to set up, and how may it be adapted for different horses?

Schooling through grids is the most useful jumping exercise that riders can perform. When schooling youngsters, grids help to establish a consistent stride, and are useful for all horses needing to improve rhythm and straightness.

First, riders must find out how many of their own strides equate to one stride of their horse. A rough guide is three or four human strides to every equine canter stride, though this will obviously depend on the size of the horse. Riders may either pace out a distance known to be a certain number of their horse's strides, or start with three of their own strides and have an assistant adapt the poles as necessary.

Canter poles are most helpful to start a grid, set at one canter stride apart. To pace out canter strides down the long side of the school, the rider should place a pole on the ground at his every third stride; about five poles is usually most suitable for a grid exercise. The horse should walk over these to begin with, and ideally will achieve three consistent walk steps in between. An assistant can then move the poles closer together or further apart, depending on how the horse manages the distances. It is a good idea to trot and canter the horse over the poles too, so the assistant can move them as necessary before jumping commences; some horses have long walk strides and short, choppy, canter strides, in which case the ground poles should fit the canter stride.

HOW TO DO IT

The first exercise may involve raising the poles at one end alternately, then asking the horse to walk and trot over them on both reins. This will encourage him to pick his feet up and establish a good rhythm. If he is calm and sensible he may do the exercise in canter too, but this may be best left until the jumps are in place and his rhythm comes from jumping.

Next, the last pole may be raised to a small cross-pole; this shape

A basic grid of a ground pole, to two cross-poles set at a bounce distance apart, then one short stride to a small upright.

encourages the horse to aim for the centre of the jump. He may be kept in trot on the approach to the last jump, but if he chooses to canter his rhythm should not be disrupted. Again, this must be ridden on both reins, the jump being changed, and placed at the end of the grid each time. The grid may be gradually built up, so that the third out of the five poles is made into a cross-pole. The horse will get one stride in between the last two jumps, making it a one-stride double. The next stage is to make the first pole a jump, so the grid is now a one-stride treble. The jumps must be kept low, as height is not yet the issue; the horse should be jumping out of his stride, as if the fences were just raised poles.

Once the horse maintains a good rhythm on both reins, the remaining two poles (numbers two and four) may be made into small jumps or just raised off the ground a few inches. The horse will now be jumping bounces – that is, every landing point is also the take-off point for the next jump. He will find this exercise tiring, so limit your grid jumping sessions to twenty minutes – any longer and the horse may tire and make mistakes.

Once the grid is set up there are many possible variations: for instance, the last jump may be raised to an upright, or perhaps the middle one – this should prevent the horse rushing to the last fence. The second and fourth jumps may be removed so the horse has to find his stride without relying on the poles. All the jumps may be raised, or perhaps raised alternately. A rider should assess his horse's progress and decide which exercise will suit him best.

The grid will be set up for the individual horse's stride, and will be unsuitable for another unless it has a similar stride. Adapting it to suit is only a case of moving the poles a few inches either way. A more experienced horse and rider may use a grid which is slightly too long or short in order to teach the horse to lengthen or shorten his stride. However, this must only be attempted once the horse has become well established in stride and rhythm.

A cross-pole encourages the horse to jump the middle of the fence, and so to stay straight all the way down the grid.

Gymnastic jumping is also very good for the rider, as it improves his balance and suppleness. One useful exercise is to remove the stirrups and ride a low grid without them, making sure not to hang onto the reins. On a reliable schoolmaster the rider's reins may be knotted and rested on the horse's neck, the rider stretching the arms forwards and riding by balance alone. This last exercise should be carried out in the safe confines of a riding school, and with an instructor or friend present; it should not be carried out while schooling alone.

Home course-building

PROBLEM Some horse owners are lucky enough to be able to give their horses the best that money can buy, ensuring their schooling takes place over the smartest showjumps. How can less well off owners get the best out of their horse's ability if they cannot afford 'proper' jumping equipment?

When the horse learns to jump it is very important that he feels he is in a safe environment, and does not risk being alarmed by, say, a wobbly wing, or getting hurt on a projecting nail. However, making jumping equipment can be very rewarding and enjoyable, *providing* safety is paramount, and anyone with a little ingenuity and some common sense can construct adequate wings and fillers at little or no cost.

CONSTRUCTION The first requirement must be poles: these will be used for many years and will need to be sturdy and weather proof, so if there is one piece of equipment worth saving for, then it is poles. For a decent jumping grid riders will need around ten poles, and for a small course of jumps perhaps the same number again. To acquire sturdy wooden poles may cost the same price as forty bales of hay or a second-hand saddle, a large amount of money to part with. However, although light wooden poles can be bought at around half the price of good solid ones, they are inferior in quality and break easily; also they often dry out in summer. If owners can afford even a few good quality wooden poles, they will be an investment.

Of course much can be gained by shopping around: thus, ready-painted but expensive poles may be bought from the local saddler, but cheaper rustic poles may be obtainable from a local wood merchant. It may even be possible to strike a deal, the owner allowing the merchant to exercise the horses, or offering to do some free work in return for some poles. After all, there is nothing to lose by asking!

As an alternative to poles, the middle section of carpet rolls may be used, the kind kept in bulk at furnishing warehouses; lengths of household drainpipe are also a possibility. Both of these are plastic based, and will need to be weighted inside with sand so they are not knocked down too easily. Carpet-roll inner tubes are usually discarded by the manufacturers and are both cheap and hard-wearing; drainpipes on the other hand are quite flimsy and really a last resort, but are cheap and readily available. These may be painted to look more colourful; they may also be used in conjunction with manufactured plastic sheets, available from certain mail-order catalogues and tack shops. These depict walls, flowers or patterns and are placed over the poles so they hang down in front of the jump as a 'filler'.

Wooden wings are certainly available at great expense, but can be created by a handy craftsman or carpenter out of planks of wood cheaply purchased. Empty oildrums are useful for placing poles on, but have their limitations regarding height and stability. They are available from some garages at little or no cost, and come in varying sizes. They should be clean and in good condition, and may be weighed down with sand or liquid for extra stability. It is possible to weld supports to the larger metal drums, for placing the poles on. However, if these are not detachable they must be turned away from the horse when not in use.

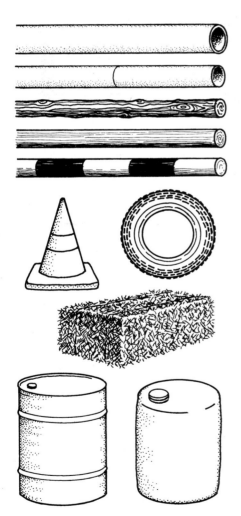

The raw materials from which to construct your fences: cardboard tubes from the inside of carpet rolls, an assortment of poles, traffic cones, tyres, straw bales, oil drums and plastic water barrels

Sharp-eyed owners will start to see many discarded objects as potential equipment, from plastic cones to tyres. Providing the jumps are solid and safe, it is possible to construct amazing courses from the barest minimum. In fact, the horse which learns to jump over a real variety of fences will be more worldly wise when it comes to compete, and will be less alarmed by any strange-looking jumps and obstacles that he might meet in the future.

Plastic barrels can be used on their own to make a jump

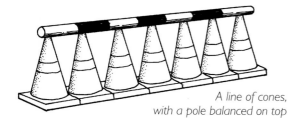

A line of cones, with a pole balanced on top

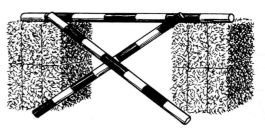

Straw bales can be used as stands for poles, and can be raised or lowered easily. They are broad enough to hold a couple of poles if required. They also make good fillers

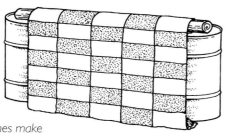

Old oil drums and traffic cones make effective stands. Here two oil drums support plastic sheeting, painted so that it resembles a wall, slung over a pole and weighted at the bottom with sand

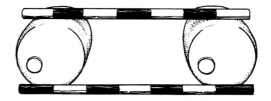

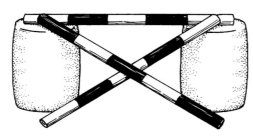

Cross-poles with upright plastic barrels; the cross-poles rest just in front of the horizontal pole (left); and (above) Two plastic barrels, laid on their side, with one painted pole balanced on top, and a second positioned just in front of the barrels to give a ground line

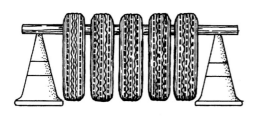

Old tyres make an effective filler; (right) slung on a pole which rests on two cones, and (above) propped up against a pole

Part 4:
COMPETITION

WORK

How to determine a horse's future

PROBLEM Is there any way of knowing if a horse will excel at any particular discipline? This is especially important when buying a horse.

SOLUTION Unfortunately there is really no way of knowing whether or not a horse will be good at something: all the right bloodlines in the world are not enough if it has an unruly temperament or a fault of conformation.

When buying a youngster for a specific purpose, there are advantages and disadvantages. Hopefully the potential buyer will be able to see at least one of the parents, maybe even in action, and if the sire and/or dam are, say, bold jumpers and have good temperaments, then the youngster will probably be a good buy as a competition horse. As with any young horse, however, how it develops is to a certain extent a gamble; but seeing the parents, or other horses from the same breeding line, will give a good indication of what to expect. Breed characteristics, too, will play a certain part: for instance, Thoroughbreds and Arabs have quick reactions but may be somewhat flighty, whereas heavyweight horses and cobs may be of a more stable temperament but less athletic.

What to look out for:

◆ *A friendly, inquisitive manner, and a bold nature.*
Good general conformation:
◆ *Matching pairs of legs, blemish-free and sturdy.*
◆ *Knees which are wide and straight, in alignment with the rest of the leg; it is vital the horse has good legs for competing, as he will be under a great deal of strain.*
◆ *Hocks which are straight and strong, capable of push-*
ing off the ground and providing momentum, and quarters broad and rounded.
◆ *A back which is compact and not dipped.*
◆ *The chest should be wide and accommodating.*
◆ *A short neck is to be preferred to a long one, although it should be well set on to the body.*
◆ *The shoulder should slope at an angle of approximately 45°; if it is too upright it will produce a choppy stride.*

Obviously it is preferable to select the offspring of a sire and dam with a known performance record, or selectively bred to excel in a certain discipline – but such horses are generally much more expensive, and the large majority of people who compete as a hobby rather than professionally will probably buy their horse from a private sale or an auction, where the horses' breeding is often not known. In this case, the potential buyer should look out for certain basic attributes in a horse; these are described in the box on the following page:

Much can be gained by looking at the horse's general carriage, how he carries his head and tail, and whether or not he has loose, free movement. As long as he has certain good points, these may well outweigh his faults, depending on what he is bought for. If he is very young and quite untried, it will be difficult to see exactly how he will turn out – but would-be buyers should remember that serious faults are unlikely to improve over the years. In the older horse which is physically developed and fully grown, it is usually possible to recognise certain attributes that will obviously lend themselves to a particular discipline.

In the UK, the Horse Database provides an invaluable service to those wishing to buy or sell competition horses. All horses registered with their respective British Horse Society affiliated groups, and also the Horse Trials group, must register their details on the Database. This will include identification and also competition achievements, which are automatically recorded. Any horse owner or breeder may, for a set fee, register their horse on the Database. It will be allocated a number, so its identity and record may be checked by anyone at any time.

Below left: This horse does not have a very strong topline, however, he has proved himself to be a good all-round riding club horse competing in dressage, showjumping and cross-country without any problems. He is kind and honest and always does all that is asked of him. A good prospect for the rider who wants to have a lot of fun in all the disciplines at Riding Club level.

Centre: A well-bred yearling just purchased from an auction. He is well put together with a clearly defined topline and strong hocks. At present his shoulder is a little upright, but youngsters can change shape dramatically from year to year, until they reach maturity at around four years of age. A good prospect for an experienced rider who perhaps wants to show in hand, and then school on for eventing.

Right: This horse has a very stong topline, a nice sloping shoulder, a good length of neck and strong hocks. On appearance he would sell himself as a good prospect for any discipline.

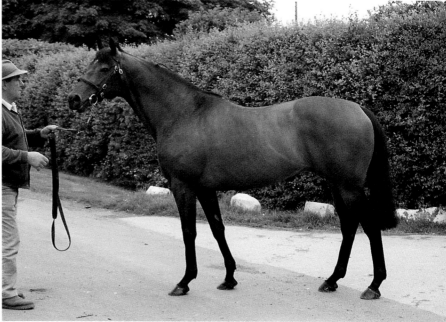

THE SHOW HORSE
Showing is perhaps the most difficult field to 'buy your way into' in this way, as most animals of show quality are bred for the purpose and very expensive – few people are lucky enough to find a beautifully made show horse without being especially selective. Of course, much will depend on the breed and the classes the handler wishes to enter; for instance, a class for hacks or utility horses is bound to include more types of horse than a specific category such as mountain and moorland.

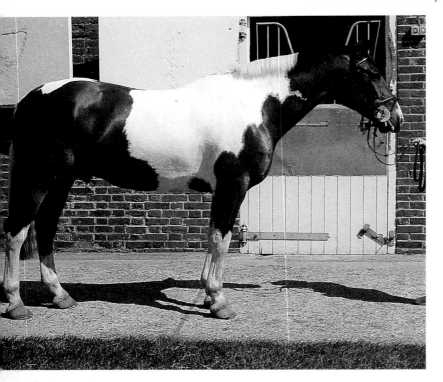

Colour is less important than courage in the potential showjumper.

THE SHOWJUMPER

The rider looking for a showjumper has the advantage in that most bold and willing horses may have the potential to succeed in that field. Also, looks are not important, so the horse with a Roman nose or splints should not be hugely disadvantaged by these. Most successful showjumpers are compact, with a short back and rounded quarters; a round croup is often referred to as a 'jumper's bump', and generally indicates powerful quarters. Legs should be tough and strong, and capable of taking the strain of competition work. Other aspects of conformation are not so important, and may be outweighed by temperament and ability.

THE EVENT HORSE
The event horse needs to be fast, brave and well built, with a tough 'leg at each corner'. The strain upon wind and limb whilst riding across country is great, and a lightweight horse may not stand up to this sort of exertion. A deep girth and wide chest suggests plenty of heart and-lung room, essential for galloping and jumping across country.

THE DRESSAGE HORSE
The dressage horse must above all move with grace, power and elegance; it should also have the potential to work in a good outline so the head must be well set on, and the quarters well developed, with strong hocks. A correctly sloping shoulder will lend itself to smooth movement, and an equable temperament to the hours of schooling preparation. Many successful dressage horses have significant continental influence – though at local level breeding is less important.

Starting in endurance riding

SOLUTION

The good thing about endurance riding is that many types of horse are capable of excelling at it, as long as they have stamina, a willing temperament and strong legs. In most horse-riding countries there are local long-distance rides that take place country-wide, leading to national and international competitions. There is not such a sense of etiquette or fashion in the endurance field as in other disciplines, and competitors may enjoy the thrill of taking part without the pressure of seeking to be placed or having to 'look the part'.

To find out about local endurance groups contact the BHS (address on page 148); they will be able to provide details of the nearest branch. Charity rides are a good introduction to endurance riding because they will only be twenty miles or so in length; they also provide a good opportunity to practise map-reading skills. It may be possible to ride with another person from the group, which is safer as well as being more enjoyable. Riders will find it useful to take a plastic map holder with them, which may be strapped around the waist and will keep the map dry, and also a compass and a stopwatch; these may be attached to the saddle for easy access, or kept in a pocket. The dress code is quite relaxed, so riders should wear something comfortable. Bear in mind that it may be necessary to remove clothing if the going gets hot, so several thinner layers are more advisable than just a couple of thick coats. The horse's saddle must be a very good fit, and it is advisable to fit a gel pad or cushioned numnah underneath to help reduce concussion and strain on the back. The rider him/herself may well need cushioning, too, so be prepared with seat-savers (cushioned saddle covers).

PROBLEM

Endurance riding is fast becoming a popular sport world-wide; so, what does the would-be competitor have to do to take part in this discipline?

Arabs and Arab-cross horses are preferred for endurance work because they are so incredibly tough.

One aspect of endurance riding that many forget is that the rider must be extremely fit, because forty or fifty miles across country will take its toll on a body that has not been well prepared. Thus it is a good idea for anyone wishing to take part in a long-distance ride to practise with friends first, hacking out for a few hours and gradually building up the fitness of both horse and rider. Another skill which is necessary for endurance riding is that of map reading, one in which it may take a while to achieve a reliable level of proficiency.

A veterinary surgeon checking the heart-rate at the halfway stage of a competition; any sign of stress and the horse will be spun — these tests are stringently observed in a competition nowadays.

When riders progress to more serious endurance rides, they will need to time themselves so they know at approximately what speed they must travel. Again, a charity or local ride is the perfect place to practise: riders should mark out the route on their map, and note the start time and maximum finish time. If the ride has checkpoints where a card is punched to confirm the rider has been past, these can be noted, together with the time of arrival and departure. If not, it may help to divide the route into sections which will help riders to keep to a timescale. Then the overall time taken to finish the ride can be compared on the map with distance and checkpoints, and this will give riders an idea of when they should reach a certain point.

Having successfully completed a local or charity ride, riders may wish to tackle longer rides. These will be of at least thirty miles and will probably have vet gates, where the horse is examined for soundness both in the limbs and heart before he continues; if his pulse is too high he may have to wait before he can continue, losing valuable time. Most endurance riders will be going at a fair pace, trotting most of the time, cantering where possible, and only walking when the ground is uneven or they are ahead of time. If there is a nice flat piece of ground to canter across, it is best to make the most of it in case there is rough ground ahead or riders lose time or get lost. It is a good idea to detail a friend to meet you at various places stationed strategically around the route, to provide water for the horse to drink, to sponge him down, and/or to provide sustenance for the rider. He/she can also take unwanted jackets, or provide more clothing if necessary.

Those riders serious about competingwill take part regularly in rides around the country; details of these will be provided by national endurance organisations, or the endurance branch of the BHS. National competitions are graded from bronze through to silver and gold, gold being the winner, and generally indicating the highest level of knowledge and experience. Some rides may involve staying over at a certain location with the horse, or travelling long distances to reach it. The more demanding the distance, the fitter the horse will need to be, and probably the faster he will need to go. This of course involves serious training, something riders should consider if they also intend holding down a job or have a family, or both.

Preparing for cross-country

'Cross-country' is a term used to cover a multitude of events, including one-, two- and three-day horse trials, hunting, hunter trials, point-to-points and team chasing. Horse trials also incorporate the disciplines of dressage and showjumping. Hunting is a seasonal bloodsport; hunter trials originated from end-of-season rides over hunting ground, and point-to-points were originally races over similar ground. A team chase is rather like a hunter trial and a race rolled into one, where teams of three or four riders compete across country for the fastest team time. As interest in cross-country riding has grown, events are held regionally on an ever-increasing scale, although the original concept of pleasure riding has been superseded by a much more competitive outlook.

PROBLEM Cross-country riding is exhilarating and enjoyable; so, what must would-be riders do if they want to take part, and what preparation is required?

SOLUTION Anyone with a bold, capable horse can take part in hunter trials and team chasing at local level, but a more talented and versatile horse is needed in order to succeed at horse trials where other disciplines are involved. The horse should be schooled over as many types of fence as possible before entering a competition, preferably taking him to a schooling day at a local course, or hiring a cross-country course for your own schooling or for private instruction. Many of the course fences will have been carefully designed and built, at great expense, and cannot hope to be matched at home by even the most ingenious horse owner. For this reason it is important that the horse has some idea of what to expect before he goes to an event, as it will be somewhat frustrating if he is eliminated at the first fence!

Once riders feel their horse is fit and experienced enough to enter an event, it is a case of finding somewhere suitable. Local riding clubs, newspapers and magazines carry information about local events, and will give details of the show secretary, from whom a schedule and entry form can be obtained. Some classes may be entered on the day, though there is usually an additional charge for this privilege. It is important when first competing to enter for classes that are well within the horse's ability, so he is not over-faced by fences bigger than he has ever met before. It is much better to take him round a small course slowly and complete it successfully, than to ride furiously for a place and risk frightening him.

As the horse progresses in ability and experience, the rider may wish to try bigger courses. It is usual for one venue to have several classes with varying fence heights, so competitors may work their way up to the bigger fences; this is similar to the system that prevails at BHTA events, where points are awarded every time horses are placed in a class, until the horse upgrades to jump bigger fences at a higher level. Horse and rider may enter at novice level and work their way up to open classes, where all the horses competing will have gained a similar number of points. They may wish to go further afield to larger events, which will require much more travelling and training, and a great deal of time. If you join the Horse Trials Association, the office will then give you details of trial dates around the country.

Dress code will depend on the event, but usually requires the following:

- *Cream or beige jodhpurs and a hacking jacket, or cross-country colours.*
- *A skull cap, back protector and gloves are essential.*
- *Long leather riding boots provide more support than rubber ones.*
- *The horse's legs must be well protected: exercise bandages or brushing boots are adequate, though competition boots which also protect the tendons, used with over-reach boots, are a more sensible option.*
- *A breastplate may be necessary to hold the saddle in place as the horse stretches over his fences and gallops up- and downhill.*
- *An over-girth fitted over the saddle will give extra security.*

There are certain pieces of tack that will not be allowed at BHS events (addresses on page 148), including draw-reins and standing martingales. It is best to check with the schedule rules, or to telephone the show secretary if in doubt as to what is allowed.

Stage fright

PROBLEM   Some horses appear to suffer from 'stage fright' when taken to shows and events, refusing to co-operate with their rider and becoming anxious or nervous. Why does this happen when they behave impeccably at home, and how can the situation be resolved?

SOLUTION   Initially a horse will almost certainly behave with huge excitement at a show, in the same way that a child behaves at Christmas or on its birthday. Even the preparations may cause him excitement, to the extent that he may break into a sweat at the sight of his travelling boots. This problem may be rectified easily if it is dealt with early enough – but if it becomes a habit it is harder to resolve.

Owners should start by making the horse's lifestyle varied and interesting – although it is advisable to have a daily routine, if it is too strict the horse may feel uncomfortable or become anxious whenever it is broken. So, providing feed and turn-out times are kept to the same, or similar, each day, owners may try varying the horse's work routine. For instance, instead of lungeing for one day, schooling for three days, jumping for one day and hacking the next, they might vary the sequence of these work sessions so the horse does not know what to expect. Otherwise he may assume that as soon as he is schooled around jumps he is going to jump, or that if he is in the school he will always do flatwork and never jump. The rider could try starting with flatwork, then introduce a few jumps at the end, thus keeping the horse on his toes and making the flatwork different and more interesting. It may also be useful to jump in the schooling area and do flatwork in the jumping paddock, just so the horse listens to the rider and cannot assume from his surroundings what he is going to be doing for that particular day's work.

Some horses get anxious during the preparations for a show, for instance as they are being plaited up, or when loading. It may therefore be helpful to take the horse on less exciting outings at various intervals throughout the year, maybe travelling him to nearby

No stage fright here! This chap obviously knows his job and is enjoying every minute of it!

woodland or schooling facilities, so that he does not always end up at a show. Hopefully he will then learn that preparations for travel are not always associated with something exciting.

It may help the horse stay calm if sometimes he is taken to a show but does not compete, letting him just take in the atmosphere, and doing nothing more exciting than riding over the practice jumps. Perhaps the rider is very competition-minded, and is himself getting anxious or wound up; he may be pushing the horse too far, asking him to jump fences that are too high, or going too fast in the ring.

If the horse is actually quite happy within his routine, his nervous tension may simply be due to the fact that he is enjoying himself so much, which is why it is only at a show that he rushes his fences and scares himself. In this case he will probably learn to calm down: the rider should work him well away from other horses, preferably in a quiet corner, and take him quietly into the ring only when his number is called – he should try to avoid waiting around in the collecting ring with other anxious horses. He should be in no rush to canter once in the ring, but instead should walk around the jumps and reassure the horse before the bell goes. Perhaps he is winding the horse up himself by flapping his legs or shortening the reins; he must therefore be careful to maintain a quiet but firm position throughout.

> *One option is to use calming herbs in the horse's diet; these are sold by most feed manufacturers as a supplement. Camomile tea is reputed to provide short-term relaxation when given to the horse the day before the show – and the rider may find it beneficial to take some, too.*

Entry requirements for cross-country competitions

SOLUTION In order to compete in an affiliated horse trial, the owner must first make sure his horse is registered on the national Database. The horse must also have an up-to-date vaccination card showing tetanus and 'flu jabs, and be registered with the Horse Trials Association. It is important to note that if owner and rider are different, they must both be registered. It is also compulsory for the rider to carry a medical card so that in the event of an accident or emergency any relevant conditions are known.

Any rider wishing to compete in a point-to-point must obtain a rider's certificate; if they also train the horse they must register as the trainer. The horse must have an up-to-date vaccination card, and also be registered with the Jockey Club. Point-to-points are run by the local hunts, and so the horse must qualify to take part by hunting with the relevant local pack. Anyone taking part in a point-to-point race will be up against stiff competition. The other competitors may well have more experience and resources at their disposal, compared with local hunter trials or riding club cross-country events where competitors are likely to be less professional.

Hunter trials and team chases also have less rigorous entry requirements, and are run on a pay-upon-entry basis. However, it is still imperative that any competing horse is regularly vaccinated against tetanus and 'flu, and riders are advised always to carry their medical details.

PROBLEM What must the would-be competitor do in order to take part in the various cross-country events?

Team chasing: an energetic sport requiring both rider and horse to be fit.

Hunting, an education?

PROBLEM Many riders take their horse hunting during the winter; is this a useful part of the horse's education, or just a thrill for riders?

SOLUTION Most equine practices have good and bad points, and the sport of hunting is no exception; ultimately it is up to the individual owner or rider to decide whether to take his/her horse. There are three types of hunting: the traditional bloodsport where a pack of hounds chases a fox, deer or hare; drag-hunting where the hounds follow a pre-laid artificial scent; or mock-hunting where the hounds follow a person whose clothes are impregnated with the scent of aniseed. All hunts take place across country, over natural obstacles and across varied terrain.

ADVANTAGES Hunting is an excellent way of introducing a horse to cross-country jumping, as he will see so many natural fences such as ditches, hedges and walls. Regular hunting is excellent for making the horse fit, and will accustom him to performing in the exciting atmosphere induced by a throng of other horses galloping about. This is rarely to be experienced at a show or event, and is something most horses will enjoy, because they have a natural herd instinct.

DISADVANTAGES The bad points will depend on the hunt, as some may be less disciplined than others; also, it is quite usual to canter or gallop along tarmac roads and uneven surfaces in the course of a day's hunting, putting enormous strain on tired legs. Furthermore there is often a lot of waiting around as the hounds work out where the quarry has gone, so the horse is getting hot and excited, and may then have to stand around for half an hour or so in the cold, running the risk of getting chilled. There is also a high risk of injury in the hunting field, as a result of falls. There are frequently loose horses and accidents, perhaps as several horses refuse a jump and riders get too close to one another.

Hunting will teach most horses to behave sensibly in company; in their competitive career they will then be more likely to settle down and concentrate when asked.

ETIQUETTE Anyone wanting to hunt must apply to the hunt secretary, as field numbers are often limited to preserve good relations with landowners for safety reasons. This involves telephoning the secretary to introduce yourself and to ask permission. On the day of the hunt it is advisable to arrive in good time and pay the day's field money or 'cap' to the hunt secretary; hunt members also subscribe annually.

Most hunts start at about 11 o'clock and go on until mid-afternoon, therefore lasting approximately four or five hours. This is, of course, a long time to be out riding, and will be quite tiring for both horse and rider; however, with a sensible outlook, riders can enjoy their day without stressing the horse too much. Many consider that it is most beneficial to keep to the back of the field so as to be able to observe the rest of the riders. This will give a general idea of the fences and how the horses are jumping them – if many are refusing a fence or stumbling on landing, there is a good chance that it is unsuitable, so avoiding action should be taken. It is always wise to keep a reasonable distance from the group of people who jump a fence together; although they are probably regular subscribers on experienced horses, there is every chance of accident or injury through kicking. (Riders with a horse that kicks will often tie a red ribbon to its tail, a useful warning in the hunting field; those with a young horse tie on a green ribbon, or tape.)

The horse must never be asked to jump more than he can manage, or to continue when he is tired; this is when he will make mistakes and stumble, even fall. At the end of the day it is generally as well to drive the horse home in a horsebox; if he is really tired he may lack concentration and stumble, or may 'tie up' – suffer an attack of azoturia – later.

DRESS FOR THE RIDER
As far as dress code is concerned, it is important to be neat and tidy, but above all safe and comfortable. Not all hunts expect their followers to dress in full hunt attire, but a skull cap or black velvet cap and gloves are essential, and a sturdy pair of long boots, preferably leather. Black is the preferred colour for hunting coats and skull cap covers, but a tweed jacket or dark-coloured waterproof clothing may be acceptable. Some hunts, however, are most particular that the correct dress is worn.

DRESS FOR THE HORSE
The horse may be well protected, as his legs will come in for plenty of strain. Supportive boots designed for competition wear offer protection to the entire lower leg and support the tendons, though they tend to rub when worn for a whole day. Over-reach boots and knee-boots will also be beneficial in some counties (for instance when jumping stone walls with North Country packs).

FIRST AID
If it is possible to carry a miniature first-aid kit this will give peace of mind, even if it is just a bandage and the veterinary surgeon's telephone number. A few plasters for the rider and change for a phone are also a good idea, as anything can happen (and usually does) when horse and rider are away from home.

THE MOCK HUNT

For the first-timer it may be best to go on a mock hunt, which will be less traditional than a fox hunt, and more laid back. The dress code and etiquette may be more relaxed, and the atmosphere one of a fun day out rather than a time-honoured sport. There will probably be fewer followers, which will give the horse a chance to accustom himself to the hustle and bustle of the 'field'.

Over-excitability

PROBLEM Horses which compete regularly are bound to be fit and on their toes, and this may lead to over-excitability. How can riders prevent the battle which often ensues at a competition?

For the horse which enjoys competing, going to an event is the highlight of his week – the adrenalin will be running and the atmosphere exciting, and it is under these circumstances that he may become somewhat exuberant. This is of course quite natural, and problems usually only occur when there is a lack of communication between horse and rider, or because of bad riding. Thus in the ring on the approach to a fence, the horse may be seen fighting the contact by shaking the head, or raising it so the rider needs to shorten the reins to gain control. This tends to make the horse fight even more, so he loses rhythm and becomes completely unbalanced. When this happens he also loses impulsion, and he will then use speed to get over the fence, a 'panic reaction' which may result in a refusal or a fall.

SOLUTION First of all the rider must question his own skills. It is likely the horse feels restricted on his approach, and does not have the freedom he needs to relax and stretch his head and neck on his approach to, and over a fence. Due to the general excitement of a show and the desire to win, many riders seem to forget the importance of good technique, and think only of getting over the fence in the quickest time. (This behaviour is seen less at 'professional' level, and mostly in young and ambitious riders who lack patience and experience.)

It is sometimes a good policy to go through all the preparations for a show – plaiting up, dressing the horse up for travel – but then just to hack quietly about when you get there. You may need to do this a few times, but eventually he should accept an outing as no cause for excitement.

The first step is to concentrate on the horse's flatwork before competing seriously again; in fact if the horse has been jumping regularly it may be worthwhile to have a complete break for a few weeks or a month. Flatwork should be taken back to basics, and it may be of benefit to have riding lessons so rider faults may be picked up; often it is difficult to spot one's own problems when concentrating on the horse. Lunge lessons may be beneficial to the rider, so he can practise maintaining his balance without leaning on the reins. It may be a good idea to be lunged on another, more docile horse, without stirrups and doing arm and shoulder exercises without the reins.

Whilst schooling the horse, the rider should concentrate on keeping him soft and minimising resistance. The horse may be uncomfortable in his mouth because the rider's hands are harsh or the bit is small and is pinching. Perhaps the rider always holds the reins too short and the horse feels he must pull against the contact – if so, the rider should try and work him in a long and low outline, so the hocks and quarters are providing impulsion but not excess speed, and the head and neck are stretched down. Transition work may be carried out like this, so the horse is not relying on rein contact alone for commands, but also the rider's weight, leg and voice aids. Ground pole exercises will prove very useful, so the horse learns to work over poles as part of the schooling process and does not always associate them with excitement and nervous strain.

The poles may be laid out singly at various points in the school, perhaps diagonally across the four corners, and the horse asked to walk, trot and canter over them without altering the rein contact or speed. The rider must drive forwards with the leg and maintain a still hand so the horse is not restricted or made tense in any way.

Once the horse will school quietly over ground poles, jumping may be introduced gradually, first by raising the poles by just a few inches. The ultimate aim is for the horse to jump the raised poles or a small fence out of his stride, without tensing up and rushing. Very low grids of three jumps may help, and if the horse needs to be restrained the rider must try to do so gently, without restricting the head. Half-halts on the rein – a give-and-take contact – are more effective than a constant pull, combined with a firm, supporting leg. If the horse tries to rush he may be turned away in a large circle and asked to approach again, and this may be repeated until he is relaxed.

Even though the re-schooling may take a long while, it will be worth all the missed opportunities of competing if horse and rider are in harmony once more; after all, nothing productive will be achieved when they are fighting all the time.

Avoid anything which will provoke undue excitement in your day-to-day schooling sessions, and frequently walk the horse about on a long rein to help him relax.

Planning for competition

PROBLEM Competing involves a great deal of preparation, time and thought on the rider's part: so, what can be gained by careful planning and forethought?

SOLUTION In the excitement of getting ready to go to a competition it is all too easy to forget something important, or to assume someone else has packed the grooming kit or looked after the lorry keys. It is sensible to make a list of the necessary tasks and items, and to go through them individually; this will save time in the long run.

PREPARING THE HORSE

Most horses are nervous of loading and travelling for the first few times, so it would be a good plan to have a little practice beforehand. Also, take him on a few short journeys before travelling further afield, so he gets used to the motion and learns to balance himself. It would be absurd to spend weeks schooling the horse, and to be looking forward to an event, only to have him refuse to load and miss his class.

Before loading, the horse should be groomed and prepared for the event, and plaited up if necessary, so if there are any problems then there will not be too much to do on arrival. If plaits are secured firmly with cotton and sprayed with hairspray, they should stay intact and this saves time at the show, particularly as the horse may be fidgeting.

The horse will need to wear protective clothing when travelling, to prevent any injury during loading or transit. His legs must be covered with either bandages or boots – when travelling long distances some owners may use both. Travelling bandages are fitted over a piece of gamgee or foam, which is wrapped around the lower leg, covering the fetlock joint and also providing a degree of

Ready for off! In winter the horse would probably need a warmer rug; he might also need a poll guard, particularly if he was likely to fidget; and a grey or a white tail would be best wrapped up in an old stocking to keep it clean.

warmth and support. Knee and hock boots may be used in conjunction with bandages to give added protection and peace of mind.

There are two types of travelling boots, short transit boots and longer quilted versions. Transit boots are often used on short journeys or on ponies, and offer minimal protection to the cannon bone. The knees, hocks and fetlock joints are largely unprotected, though when the boots are fitted over a large piece of gamgee or foam these areas may be covered. Longer travelling boots are preferable, as they are thicker and come down to the coronet band of the foot, as well as covering the knees and hocks. Another advantage is that they can be put on quickly.

The horse's tail should also be protected as it may be rubbed against a partition, or stained if the horse stales in the lorry. Tail bandages are adequate but time-consuming; stockings or tail bags are quicker and more practical, and are less likely to work a plait loose.

Travelling rugs come in various styles and weights depending on the time of year; for a long journey in winter the horse will need a heavier version so he does not catch chill, whereas in summer a sweat sheet or lightweight cover may be suitable. These offer protection against knocks and scratches, and keep the coat smooth; a sweat sheet or wicking rug will also remove any sweat from the horse's body so it is absorbed into the atmosphere.

A poll guard is also advisable, particularly if the horse is prone to pulling back or rearing. Fitted to the headcollar, these small pads are designed to take any impact and protect the sensitive poll. A tail bandage wrapped around the headpiece of the headcollar will suffice, and may be placed over foam or cotton wool.

PREPARING THE LORRY

The floor of the lorry or trailer should be prepared with clean matting or bedding, and a loop of breakable twine attached to the tying-up ring. In the morning there will be little time to carry out such tasks, as everyone will be rushing around or panicking.

TACK AND EQUIPMENT

It will be useful to have a list of items of equipment, and to tick off each one as it is loaded into the lorry, so nothing is left behind. The list may include:

- Tack and equipment for the show, including numbers, and string with which to attach them.
- A spare set of clothes and protective overalls; they will always come in handy, even if used by someone else.
- A small tack-cleaning kit for a final touch-up. A miniature grooming kit (hoof pick, hoof oil, face wipes, clean body brush), fly repellent and a plaiting kit.
- A bucket, sponge and sweat scraper with which to wash the horse down; and save space by packing the equipment into the bucket.
- Drinking water for the horse, because some water facilities may be unsuitable.
- A haynet to keep the horse occupied, and also a small feed to tempt him back onto the lorry.
- Loading equipment – lunge line, schooling whip, small feed – should be kept close to hand, and packed for the return journey just in case.
- Some spare string for emergencies.
- A set of pre-rolled bandages, to save time on the return journey.
- A first-aid kit for both horse and human.
- The veterinary surgeon's telephone number, and some change for a phone.

HIRING TRANSPORT

If hiring transport, a reputable firm should be chosen, as a breakdown could cause serious problems with the horse on board. If possible the vehicle should be taken home the day before the event so it may be disinfected and cleaned out, since any germs or infection from previous passengers could be passed on. It may also be advisable to take the vehicle out for a trial run the day before the show, because if it has not been used for some time the battery may be flat. Check that the lights and indicators work and are wired up correctly, and that the flooring and ramps have not rotted or become unstable. The petrol or diesel should also be checked and filled in advance, so there is no need to make unnecessary stops at a filling station once loaded and en route.

Looking calm and confident: obviously well prepared in his mind as well as in physical condition.

◆   A map for the journey, together with a contact number for the organisers.
◆   Details of the vehicle's height and weight should be kept in the cab in case the journey entails driving under low bridges, or over bridges with weight restrictions.
◆   Money and food for the human contingent, as event days are notoriously long.

It is advisable to leave in plenty of time, to allow for diversions or even getting lost. On arrival at the event it is a good idea to leave the horse on board if he is quiet (supervised, of course) while the rider goes to collect his number and find out where everything is. The top door of a trailer or the ramp of a lorry may be opened so that the horses can look out and see what is happening – otherwise if they can hear all the goings-on but not see them, they might really get in a panic.

Walking the course is vital, as distances and/or difficult fences will need advance planning – perhaps a different approach or a certain number of strides. The fences should also be checked in case they fall easily or are unstable. The rider will be much more confident about his ride if he has arrived without mishap and knows the course, a self-assurance which will transmit itself to the horse and make for a happier day out.

Schooling for competition

SOLUTION

As the days lead up to the horse's event he should be maintaining fitness so he is at his prime when competing. He should be in peak condition both mentally and physically – although there is a fine line between this and going stale, which of course must not be crossed. The horse may be said to be stale when, for example, he has practised his dressage test so many times that he anticipates the movements, or is blasé about his jumps and becomes careless.

Preparation for the event should have started several weeks previously, practising certain elements of a test or jumping different courses. The schooling sessions for the week before a cross-country event may be as follows:

MONDAY

Flatwork, which is of course as important as the jumping itself. The rider will be trying to bring the horse's hocks underneath him, and making sure he is listening carefully to the aids and commands. He may practise lengthening and shortening over a certain distance between two poles, adapting the horse's stride to suit the required interval. Then he might pop the horse over a few cross-poles and low jumps, concentrating on seeing a stride and altering it where necessary.

TUESDAY

More flatwork, using plenty of school movements and exercises.

One versatile exercise is to place three 13m circles along the long side of the school, laid out with cones or small oil drums. These may be ridden in sitting trot, the rider concentrating on maintaining a good rhythm throughout and working the horse in an outline. Having completed the three circles he will ask for canter in the first corner, lengthening for a few strides down the long side, then shortening and bringing the horse down to trot again before rebalancing for the circles. Again this will make the hocks work hard to propel the horse forwards correctly; it will also improve his rhythm.

WEDNESDAY

Some gridwork, beginning with a small grid of five jumps, and gradually raising the height to make the exercise more challenging. A spread may be included at the end of the grid, and plenty of bounce strides to keep the horse on his toes.

THURSDAY

Some light schooling, and repeat briefly the exercises he has done previously in the week; then out for a brisk hack. Canter up a couple of hills, allowing a short burst of gallop where it is safe: this will serve as a pipe-opener for the horse, giving him a taste of what is to come at the weekend, but not making him stale.

PROBLEM

What schooling should be done in the days leading up to an event, and also on the day before a competition?

FRIDAY Try a few cross-country fences, either by hiring a nearby course for an hour or so, or by jumping over some home-made ones. Refreshing the horse's memory with regard to water or other jumps not seen regularly will have been done in the weeks leading up to the event, though a last reminder of 'scary' or difficult jumps will always help the horse.

SATURDAY (Before a Sunday event): some light schooling, not enough to tire the horse out, but just to prevent him being like a coiled-up spring at the event, when he would lose concentration. Some riders may prefer not to ride the horse the day before, so he has more energy for the event itself. This could be the wrong decision, however, if he uses up his energy by bouncing up and down in excitement rather than going forwards.

SUNDAY Once the horse arrives at the show on the Sunday, it is important that he is settled, both mentally and physically, before he competes. If he is to perform at his best he must have recovered from the journey to the show, be warmed up enough so as not to risk muscle strain, and alert with his mind on the job in hand. If he is quiet he might stay on the lorry for a few minutes while the rider sorts out entries, numbers and his start-time; if not, he may be walked round with a lightweight rug on, to calm down and take in his surroundings – he may be allowed to graze a little if the class is not imminent, as this will keep him from fidgeting and should reassure him.

There is no point in warming up the horse too soon, so if there is time in hand, again, he may be led around the show ground so he can have a good look at everything. It is wise to begin warming him up about forty minutes before his start time – twenty minutes loosening up, walking and trotting, and twenty minutes lightly schooling. This will involve circles in walk and trot within sight and earshot of the start so he is thoroughly loosened up, and to keep him calm. He should be allowed to stretch his head and neck down, and may be allowed a short canter if he is not too excited. He should also pop over the practice jump a few times to help him 'get his eye in'; ideally, by the time he has done all this it will be just about time for him to start, so that he does not 'wind down' or have to wait about before he sets off round the course.

Gridwork will help to keep him interested and 'snappy'.

Coping with cross-country obstacles

SOLUTION Before the rider attempts any kind of cross-country riding, he must be fully in control of his horse on the flat, as the terrain may be sloping or uneven, requiring a good deal of skill and balance. Cross-country riding is possibly the most risky of the equine disciplines, simply because the horse is going faster and the obstacles are solid, so the likelihood of falling is higher. Also the riding area is larger and less enclosed, so the horse may behave less predictably.

The main thing is to stay effective and in control: a pretty jumping position is of no use at all if the rider is promptly hit on the nose by the horse's head, and then carted off across the field. 'Bridging' the reins may help the rider to maintain his balance – this involves looping each rein into the opposite hand, so there is a double piece of rein with which to lean on the neck. He must also learn to maintain a deep, secure seat so that he can adapt his position to suit the fence and approach; the person who appears to be 'glued' to the saddle will be more effective than one who perches on his knees and bounces about.

So, what type of fences may be encountered, and how should they be ridden?

THE LOG OR BRUSH

For this sort of straightforward fence the rider must be ready to give with his hands and 'fold' sufficiently so he stays in balance over the fence, though not so much that he is off the saddle and easily unseated. In showjumping the fences are generally higher and more upright, and so the rider needs to 'fold' his upper body forwards to a greater degree in order to lift his weight further off the saddle thus enabling the horse to make a good bascule. The cross-country rider needs to be more secure because he will be moving faster and the horse may land more heavily and less predictably because of the different types of obstacles.

PROBLEM Competing in trials and events across country involves jumping various obstacles that require a different approach or style of riding. What fences may be encountered, and how should they be ridden?

The horse is descending very tentatively, but the rider is deep and secure in the saddle, and giving him every chance to gain in confidence.

THE DROP FENCE As might be imagined, the landing side is much lower than the take-off side. Often at a field boundary the level of one side is naturally lower, or the drop may have been purpose-built so the horse runs up a small hill in order to jump down the other side.

Don't be tempted to tip forward as your horse drops down the steps. Sit up and lean back to stay in balance.

STEPS

Here the horse jumps up or down several levels: three is usual – four is much more difficult – and the deeper the step, the more severe the test.

On the approach it is important to sit deep in the saddle well before the take-off point, because the horse's trajectory is more steeply upwards or downwards, and when jumping steps there is considerable deceleration which the less experienced rider may find unseating. The rider must stay in the centre of gravity, which involves sitting up, rather than tipping forwards as the horse jumps. On landing the reins must be allowed to slip through the hands (although be careful not to let go altogether) so he may use his head to balance himself unhindered. For any drop, the landing will be steep, so the rider must adapt his position and lean back to stay in balance.

It is quite acceptable to hold a piece of mane to help you balance as the horse jumps, at least until you get used to the feeling of deceleration and the change in gravity. The weight should be firmly in the heel – in fact pushing the lower legs slightly forwards will offer a more secure position. Once the horse has landed the reins should be collected up quickly, and the normal cross-country position resumed.

BANKS

Natural banks are not often seen at events, most being artificially constructed, dome-shaped and moulded into the ground. They are often steeper on the descent, and may have a small jump or ditch on the landing side. As the horse approaches the take-off side of the bank, he will need to have a short, bouncy stride; if it is too long his trajectory will be flat and he may risk catching a forefoot on the edge of the bank as he jumps up onto it. The rider must 'fold' sufficiently to stay with the horse's momentum, but he should be careful not to get his head in the way should the horse raise his own excessively; he may find it helpful to hold it to one side to avoid getting knocked in the teeth. Once on top of the bank he should sit up as soon as possible, because the landing side will come along sooner than he thinks! A simple descent down a bank is similar to a drop, in that the rider should lean back as the horse jumps down. However, if there is a ditch on the landing side he should be ready to give the horse a kick to encourage him over it, and he must be sure to have his weight in his heel or he may be left behind and risk being unseated.

DITCHES

Ditches are normally constructed by the course builder, and are therefore built up on the inside walls and so very well defined and sound. Natural ditches may be less reliable on the take-off and landing, and should be approached more slowly in case the edges crumble under the horse and rider's weight. It is normally best for the horse to decide where to take off at a ditch, the rider simply maintaining the impulsion at a steady pace; he should also be prepared for the horse to have a spook and a good look, and to jump in a rather ungainly way – he may well get left behind, and should get ready to go 'with' the horse rather than to fold as such. On landing, the horse will almost certainly need to use his neck to balance, so the rider may need to let the reins slip so that his stride is not impaired.

WATER

Water jumps present all manner of combinations, the simplest being either a slope or a small drop in, and a step or slope up the other side. A water complex should be approached in a controlled trot or canter – depending how experienced (or not) the horse is – but with *plenty* of impulsion: too little will risk an untidy take-off and the horse pecking, and a ducking into the bargain! Go too fast, and the drag of the water as the horse lands may cause him to pitch on his nose. A short stride with plenty of impulsion is always preferable, to maintain the forward momentum and so help the horse keep his feet and get out the other side. If there is a drop it should be jumped as such, though a slope may be ridden with a normal cross-country seat and a very firm leg. If on the way out the horse has to jump up a step, this should be approached with plenty of impulsion, otherwise he will risk stumbling up it and unseating his rider.

It is better to leave the horse to sort out how many strides he puts in as he goes through the water, rather than trying to ride for the number you may have paced it out to be. This is because it is impossible to quantify the effect that the drag of the water will have on the horse's forward progress – so let him sort it out, and just make sure he does so with plenty of energy!

Your horse will cope with ditches and water jumps much more confidently if he is introduced to them as part of his training as a youngster (see also Water Shyness p14).

Safety on bad ground

PROBLEM

The competition rider will experience various terrains and changing ground conditions – how may he prepare himself, and what should he do to look after himself and the horse over bad ground?

SOLUTION

Adverse ground conditions are mainly caused by the weather, and are part of the package of riding; moreover they will be encountered all the time, and not just when competing. Horses react to the going in different ways, some liking it hard, some soft, perhaps influenced by their temperament, perhaps because of their physical shape. Racehorses in particular will favour certain ground conditions.

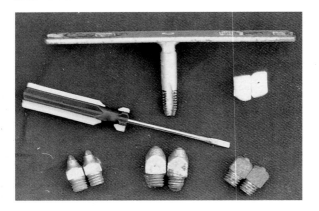

Various studs may be fitted to the horse's shoes to provide added grip, although they should not be used as an excuse to go too fast. They are screwed into the stud holes in the shoes, and come in various shapes and sizes according to the conditions and hardness of the ground. Small pointed studs will give more grip by digging into the surface on very hard ground. If conditions are worse and include wet and boggy areas, larger studs with a greater surface area may be necessary, though these may unbalance the horse if he is not used to them. Such studs should only be used at the event itself, and in the meantime the holes should be plugged with oiled cotton wool, which may be pushed in and taken out using a horseshoe nail. A tap may be used to re-thread the hole if necessary, to ensure the studs are fitted securely. This is done with a spanner, and best carried out on flat ground – it is easy to drop the studs, which may roll away or get lost in a deep bed.

HARD GROUND

Hard ground often occurs in hot, dry weather, and horses should not be expected to work on it for long periods of time; they run the risk of jarring feet and limbs, and if they are thin soled or have particularly tender feet they will almost certainly be uncomfortable. Flat hard ground is bad enough, but rutted hard ground is worse, and there is no question but the horse must be taken very steadily. If the course is timed, the rider is left with a difficult decision to make: either he must avoid going fast, or he must withdraw from the competition altogether so as not to risk the horse.

SLIPPERY GROUND

This often occurs at the take-off to fences when a lot of rain, and also wear and tear from pounding feet, have made an area muddy. Ice and frost will also cause slipping – though horses should not be ridden at all on ground this dangerous. In the first situation, when jumping, the rider should approach steadily and, as always, with impulsion, trying to avoid the spot that is very poached, perhaps taking a line slightly to one side of it. The horse should be allowed to find his own stride and take-off point, and the rider must be ready to go with him.

Studs may be fitted to the horse's shoes and will provide added grip. Tarmac roads may also become slippery; road studs may be screwed in, and if part of the roads and tracks phase of an event is along tarmac, it should be tackled very carefully, and the time lost made up on better going.

MUDDY GROUND

Always hard work for any horse, heavy clay and deep mud will have a considerable slowing effect. Ploughed fields are a prime example, and the rider will risk damaging the horse's tendons if he rides him too fast across plough. Some horses move through heavy ground quite successfully, while others get stuck and find it very hard work. The rider should sit quietly, but keeping the horse up together with leg and hand so as to maintain impulsion, and making sure that if he has to jump, the approaching strides are short and he does not stand off from the fence and so risk straining his legs.

Coping with competitions

SOLUTION When showjumping, having finally made it into the arena, riders need not assume it will then be all plain sailing! Unfortunately horses are unpredictable creatures, and the excitement of travelling and the other horses crowding around the showjumping ring may cause the horse to lose attention, which even for a split second could be a disadvantage. The rider should keep his horse as calm as possible; no cantering round and round the collecting ring and winding him into a frenzy. Plenty of calm words and pats on the neck will reassure him, as will working in a quiet corner away from other horses.

PROBLEM Horses often behave perfectly well at home, yet cannot cope with the excitement of competition and become spooky and 'gassy'. How does the rider sort out this problem?

The horse may find the diversions are all too much, and refuse or run out from the fences. To a certain extent this can be avoided by getting him used to imposing fences and the bustle of an event by taking him out frequently. Even if he only walks around a few times to take in the atmosphere and get accustomed to the sounds from the loudspeaker, it will be beneficial. However, if the horse is still 'spooky' once in the ring, the rider must aim to calm him down and approach the fences quietly but with impulsion. A chance of being placed is not as important as gaining the horse's trust, so there is no point in aiming for a fast time. He should be allowed to find a comfortable stride, and trotted if necessary in

There are a lot of sights and sounds for your horse to cope with at a show and he will benefit greatly if you allow him to take it all in in his own time

between fences. It is better to retire from the ring having jumped several fences calmly, than be eliminated without having the opportunity to finish on a good note.

If the horse begins to rush his fences or becomes clumsy, more work needs to be done at home to improve his schooling. All that can be done in the ring is to keep him calm and approach the fences quietly and correctly, maintaining balance and rhythm and asking him to pick his feet up, perhaps giving a little tap with the whip to keep his mind on the job.

If there is a clear-round jumping ring, it may be useful to practise in there if the horse persists in misbehaving. It is important to ride firmly and authoritatively, but at the same time trying to instil confidence in the horse. He may just need a firm hand to help him regain his concentration (see also Stage fright, page 120).

Fit to compete

PROBLEM   Before competing it is important that riders make sure their horses are fit enough to work to the best of their abilities, and so avoid the risk of straining themselves. So, how should they go about this?

SOLUTION   The amount of fitness work necessary to bring the horse to peak condition will of course depend on his existing state of fitness. For this purpose we will assume that he is in light work, but that he needs to develop muscle and improve his stamina for his forthcoming events. (We shall also assume the horse will be participating in all sorts of competitions, and that he is specifically aiming to go to a horse trial which of course involves three disciplines.)

ROADWORK   The horse can be trained whilst out hacking, as the varying terrain will bring different benefits: thus the tarmac roads will 'harden' the legs so they can withstand the concussion and strain of jumping and galloping, and hills and valleys may be used to great effect for strengthening the hindquarters and building up stamina. Note that although an indoor school or outdoor arena is suitable for flatwork and jump

Roadwork is an important part of the horse's preparation, although too much, and at too fast a trot, will cause jarring. And a jolly canter is always good to clear the wind and lift the spirits!

training, it will do nothing towards hardening the horse in preparation for his competitions, particularly if the surface is very soft and springy.

In the course of a serious fitness programme the horse may be worked six days a week, having one day off to relax and take life easy. He may be taken out for a hack two or three times a week, trotting where it is safe to do so, preferably on quiet roads when he won't have to keep stopping and starting for traffic to pass. Brisk walking is also beneficial as it tones up many separate muscles; it should be alternated with trot work at approximately ten-minute intervals, so the horse does not tire. Several short bursts of canter along a suitable piece of ground will serve as a 'pipe-opener', though he must be kept at a steady pace, and not be allowed to race off at his own speed. Flat or uphill ground is most suitable, as cantering downhill may run the risk of muscle or tendon strain, particularly when he accelerates.

FLATWORK

In his flatwork the horse should be given progressively more demanding exercises, so he is using his quarters and improving his balance and rhythm, as well as increasing his stamina. For instance, he may begin his flatwork with just walk and trot work (allowing for rests), riding an exercise of circles and figure-eights which decrease and increase in size. Gradually a canter on both reins may be introduced within the exercise, and this can be built up as the horse becomes fitter, so that eventually the work is mainly in trot and canter.

Aspects of the disciplines in which the horse will be competing should be practised, such as certain movements of a dressage test, or jump combinations that might be met with in the showjumping arena.

INDIVIDUAL FITNESS PROGRAMME

The exact fitness programme will depend on the horse's original fitness, and riders must use their common sense when deciding for how long to ride him at any one time. The horse which has been turned out to grass will take approximately twelve weeks to get reasonably fit, so riders must first estimate their own horse's stage of fitness. If he is halfway there, and in medium work that does not tax him greatly, riders may begin more demanding fitness work, so that by the time the event occurs in six weeks' time, the horse will be performing to his best ability.

It is most important to make all fitness work gradual, building on a certain aspect of the horse's schooling. Hill work is very good for the horse and may be done regularly, building up the amount of time and asking the horse to work properly, with plenty of forward energy, and containing the impulsion within his rhythm.

FEEDING FOR FITNESS

Of course all fitness work requires additional exercise, and this must be catered for in the horse's diet: he must have sufficient body fuel to cope with the additional work, and his diet should be constantly adjusted to correspond with his changing workload. An equine nutritionist will be able to advise on this matter, as it is vital that the horse has all the correct nutrients to enable him to perform to the best of his abilities.

Won't gallop

PROBLEM Many horses are very eager to follow others in a gallop when out hacking, but persuading them to gallop in good style in the show-ring can be quite difficult. Is this simply because horses are herd animals and like to run together, and if so, how can a horse be taught to gallop by the rider's aids alone?

SOLUTION A reluctance to gallop is not usually too serious a problem. First, in a showing situation there is no need for the horse to gallop flat out. What the judge requires is to see the horse lengthening his stride smoothly and in a balanced fashion – in fact, a long flowing stride will earn far more points than a quicker but more choppy one. In this respect, if a horse's gallop is his weakest pace, then it is far better to show him in an extended canter than for the rider to be seen kicking and flapping to make him go faster.

At home the horse should be worked upsides another horse in gallop, and then encouraged to overtake. Varying his work so that it includes jumping, schooling and work in hand will also help to keep him interested. And if he is just being lazy, then a quick flick with the schooling whip in order to reinforce the gallop aid may be needed until he gets the idea, or the rider may need to wear a pair of blunt spurs.

Once the horse will gallop out on a hack, he should be encouraged to do so in the paddock at home. While he will probably follow the others in the ring at a show, he will still be required to gallop alone when the judge rides him, so all his training should be conducted with a view to sharpening him up. Perhaps in the past he was allowed to 'switch off' when he was ridden, maybe always being taken on the same ride. Whenever he is ridden the

Your horse may be happy enough to gallop alongside other horses when out hacking, but remember that he'll be on his own when the judge rides him in the ring. If your paddock has a good pot-hole free surface, get in some practise at home.

Concentrate on achieving a good, quality gallop: galloping isn't just about speed! Encourage the horse to lengthen to give the appearance of gliding across the ground

horse should therefore be walked, trotted, cantered and galloped at a different place each time so he will not anticipate what is coming next, and this should help to keep him on his toes. This way of conducting his basic training both in the school and out on hacks will improve his sharpness.

Generally, the repetitiveness of showing will help the horse to accept that he must gallop when asked, and the more he does it, usually the more he will like it. In fact, the gallop is usually the most troublesome part of the show because the horse comes to anticipate it and tries to cut the corner in order to have his turn!

Competition confidence

SOLUTION Pulling a horse away from fences during a competition is a sure way of teaching him to refuse, and is a habit which must be avoided at all costs. Nevertheless, while it is important to preserve the horse's boldness, he must also be taught to jump safely. The first thing to do is to set up a series of grids at home with fairly short distances between the elements: 2.7m (9ft) at trot; 3.6m (12ft) at canter. In this way the horse learns to be athletic, adjusting his own stride without the rider's help. (Note that the distances should be adapted to suit the height of the fences and the horse's length of stride.) To start with, the fences should be no more than 0.80m (2ft 6in), and because gridwork is demanding of the horse he should be sufficiently warmed up prior to jumping.

Once both horse and rider are jumping in a safe rhythm over these grids in the school, canter work can begin over a course of fences in a small field. If the horse begins to rush a fence, he should be allowed to jump it, but should then be brought to a halt soon after landing. This should be repeated after every fence until the horse learns to anticipate the halt, which in turn will slow him up on the approach. This procedure really does work well, and horses soon learn to control their rhythm. However, in the first instance the rider must be committed to jumping the fence.

Once the horse is jumping safely at home, he should be taken to a cross-country course for a schooling session. Here the same rules apply: if he starts to rush, he must be allowed to jump but should be pulled to a halt soon afterwards – he will soon realise that what you have taught him at home must also be applied during competitions. Once he anticipates the halt he can gradually be allowed to canter away from the fence in a steady rhythm.

PROBLEM To jump cross-country courses both horse and rider must be committed: thus a bold jumper which really attacks his fences needs a bold rider to go with him. However, if the horse comes into his fences too quickly it can be a nerve-racking experience for the rider, and may cause him to pull the horse away from the fence at the last minute, rather than kicking on to jump it. This can cause the horse to lose confidence and he may then start to stop. How can both horse and rider get it together so that they are jumping boldly as a team?

Such a horse may require a little reminder from time to time, but often a good check after a fence will prompt a steadier approach at the next one, preserving both horse and rider's safety at a competition without losing valuable time when it really matters.

Showjumping for all

PROBLEM Showjumping is becoming increasingly popular with riders of all abilities; so, how should the horse be trained and prepared for this particular discipline?

Most horses love their jumping, and their riders find it an enjoyable part of the schooling process. However, taking it up as a regular sport involves a good deal of training, and a horse with natural competence and an aptitude for competing – although having said that, as with most sports, showjumping has various levels of ability, so anyone can have a go and find out his own talents and limitations.

SOLUTION The first requirement is to give the horse a solid grounding in the basics, so he has very good balance and rhythm. If he is to compete successfully he must also trust his rider, which he will only do if the rider is able to establish a sensitive relationship with him. Although some people can afford to buy their way to success, this is not an option for most of us, besides which to succeed with your own, probably quite ordinary horse as a result of patient schooling and dedication can be enormously satisfying.

In order to jump correctly the horse will need to be very well balanced and fluent on the flat, and be very supple and attentive. This may be achieved by working through the normal school movements, with frequent transitions, and working the horse in a round outline with his quarters beneath him, providing the impulsion: this is the motor, the power that will propel the horse off the ground on the take-off to a jump, so it is not a stage in the schooling process that should be neglected.

Once the horse is responding well on the flat, he may be introduced to gridwork which will teach him to jump out of his stride, help him maintain a good rhythm and develop his athleticism and style. Much can be gained by schooling the horse over a grid of small jumps, as jumping a single fence time after time becomes boring, and may result in him becoming lazy or careless. Initially a simple grid is used, with five jumps at one canter stride apart. If we assume the horse's usual canter stride is an average 9ft (2.7m), the grid will have to be at least 36ft (11m) long, with room for a straight approach and a getaway of several strides. If the schooling area is not large enough, a smaller grid consisting of either three or four jumps (18ft and 27ft/5.4 and 8.1m in length respectively) will suffice. Once the horse has completed this grid successfully on an even stride, it may then be adapted to suit a specific schooling problem.

For instance, if the horse has a habit of dragging his hindlegs or not using them properly, the grid may be shortened or a few bounce strides introduced so that he is obliged to really propel himself forwards and use his hocks. An additional bounce fence may be added in between two jumps of one canter stride (9ft/2.7m) apart. Thus the distance will be 4.5ft (1.3m), and the horse's landing point will also be the take-off point for the next fence.

The fences may be brought closer together to encourage the horse to shorten his stride, but make sure that the distance between them is realistic. As a rough guide you should assume that the horse is

Competitions are so often 'won at home', as the saying goes, and introducing the green horse to spooky fences is one of the trainer's first responsibilities.

capable of shortening or lengthening by a foot either way; thus a shortened grid of five fences will be 32ft (9.7m) in length. By the same token the grid may be lengthened by a foot to encourage the horse to stretch a little more over his fences, cover more ground and maintain impulsion without speed. The new lengthened grid of five fences will run for 40ft (12.2m). It is important to bear in mind that a change in stride is demanding for the horse, particularly when the stride is lengthened. Therefore it may be best to work on a smaller grid until the horse can complete it successfully, so he is not strained or overfaced.

Different fences may be introduced into the grid for variation, for example a parallel to encourage a good bascule, or a spread to ensure a stretch over the fence. It is important to remember that the horse will land approximately half a stride away from the fence, and he will cover more ground over a spread than an upright – therefore the next jump should be a full stride away, and paced out from the highest point of the previous jump, not the first pole.

It will also be beneficial to broaden the horse's education by showing him as many brightly coloured and unusual fences as possible, because course builders often construct some imposing-looking jumps.

To begin with, riders will probably compete locally in unaffiliated events run by riding clubs or yards or the hunt or village; these are advertised in the local press. These shows provide the perfect grounding for prospective showjumpers as they feature so much noise and bustle and offer all sorts of novice classes, starting with clear round jumping. Schooling days at showgrounds are also beneficial, as they allow the horse to see and jump different fences without the pressure of a competition.

When horse and rider are competing successfully at unaffiliated shows, it is time to move on to the next challenge, generally affiliated competitions – that is, run to the rules and specifications as laid down by the national governing body for showjumping in the particular country (addresses on page 148); it is necessary to contact these with regard to qualifying shows in the individual area. Horses are graded according to prize money won, starting with novice classes where the horse must not have won more than a certain amount of money. Horses compete at a certain level until they reach the specified winnings limit for that level, and then they upgrade. The fences become more demanding the higher the grade of the class, requiring increasing talent and versatility from both horse and rider. Many riders whose horses are of a higher grade will be competing every weekend at qualifying shows across the country, and will accumulate a lot of prize money. However, this does not mean that showjumping is necessarily a lucrative career, as the day-to-day expenses are very high.

It is not often that top British riders are seen jumping at County shows, but when they are the competition is considerably enhanced.

Risks against the clock

SOLUTION   Much will depend on the rider's level of experience, and more importantly the physical make-up and temperament of the horse. At a professional level both horse and rider will have a heightened sense of intuition gained from competing extensively, and this will tell the rider when he may take a risk – for instance, when he can ask the horse to stand off at a big spread, or ask for a burst of speed when the horse is tired.

At most competitions the course will be timed, or at least a section of it. Different organising bodies have different rules, but optimum times are generally calculated on the basis of dividing course length by the ground covered per minute. The optimum time over a novice course will be slower than over a more difficult course, as the horses and riders at higher levels will be expected to complete in a faster time. Ground conditions will also affect the time, as on a rainy day the optimum time may be increased to reduce the risk of accidents. There will also be a time limit, but unless the horse has fallen or taken the wrong route this should not pose a problem. At some events organisers may have decided upon a time representing a good, steady pace; this is known as the 'bogey time', and there is usually a prize for the combination which completes nearest to it. For the most part, however, the aim is to complete the course as quickly as possible, incurring minimum faults.

As previously stated, the horse's physical make-up will have a considerable influence on his average speed and limitations; the Thoroughbred is obviously fast, with a long, ground-covering stride, whereas a more cobby sort will need extra speed to compensate for his short stride. A very highly strung horse is probably best kept at a steady pace, as he may lose concentration and get too excited if he is asked to make up extra time and go faster.

The rider must know his horse's own capabilities: whether or not he can trust him to stay true to a line, and so cut a corner and go for a difficult angle over a fence – and whether he can trust him not to bolt if he tries to save time by galloping to the bottom of the hill without a pull. A general rule is: if in doubt, don't take the risk.

The most sensible policy is to take the whole course at a steady pace, so the horse can jump out of his stride without any problems; at novice events this speed is approximately 525m a minute. On a long straight stretch of the course the horse can be asked to lengthen his stride and cover more ground, so he makes up extra time; it is better to have a few seconds in hand and so be able to finish at a steady pace, rather than having to push the horse to his limits to make the time at the end. Riders should wear a stopwatch and note the optimum time, so they can monitor their speed and work out if they are going too fast or too slowly.

PROBLEM   When competing, what risks are involved in riding against the clock, and how do riders decide when to take them?

Going for it! Not many horses tuck up their hindlegs as well as this one, but the rider knows he does and can therefore take a chance and turn sharply as she lands – a less 'tidy' horse would take the back pole with him.

Safety must always be paramount in the rider's mind, and studs should be fitted to the horse's shoes to provide more grip – it is unwise to go too fast on wet and slippery ground, and often better to go for a safe clear round than a fast, risky one.

Dressage for all

PROBLEM Dressage once seemed an élitist sport, but is now enjoyed by a growing number of riders. How does one go about preparing the ordinary horse to take part in dressage competitions?

Dressage is judged on a points system, awarded according to how well horse and rider execute a test made up of school movements; tests are available from Preliminary to Prix St Georges levels, although riders may only be concerned with the lower levels to begin with, as progression to a higher level demands enormous skill and plenty of time spent on an exceptional horse.

The very word 'dressage' often frightens riders into thinking of fancy movements and expensive horses, perhaps putting them off competing with their seemingly imperfect mounts. However, dressage is accessible to everyone, and does not necessarily require a horse with the presence and style of a ballerina. After all, dressage is really no more than the flatwork and schooling that riders do at home anyway, a test of the responsiveness and obedience of the horse. Certainly the horses that are used purely for dressage are particularly well moving and graceful, but any well behaved horse with a soft mouth and good paces may develop into a proficient dressage performer at a lower level.

SOLUTION Flatwork is the basis of all dressage, and must be carried out sensitively. The dressage horse is trained to be very responsive to the rider's aids, and will rarely misbehave or evade whilst he is working, as he knows when to concentrate on his work, and when to relax or play. For this reason he is generally exceptionally obedient, and will have learned to respond to the rider's slightest aid.

This obedience training begins at the handling stage, when the horse learns to stand quietly or move away from the trainer when asked. He should lift his feet for picking out when requested, and lead in hand at the handler's shoulder. Vocal commands are important at this stage too, and will come into play even more when the horse is lunged. On the lunge he will learn to respect the lunge whip, and this in turn will prepare him for the rider's use of a schooling whip, which when he is schooled on the flat will teach him to react more quickly to the rider's leg aids.

Transitions and school exercises will improve the horse's balance and outline, which must be round and relaxed, and his way of going soft and loose in the dressage arena. The rider must maintain a steady contact and really drive the horse forwards, so all the impulsion is contained within his hands. Above all the dressage horse will have a consistent rhythm and good paces, which will only be developed by regular and careful schooling. It is a good idea to have lessons from an instructor, particularly when schooling an inexperienced horse when riding faults may easily creep in and become habit. The stirrup length is much longer for dressage than for day-to-day hacking, so the rider's leg is wrapped around the horse; his body should be straight and still, and in harmony with the horse.

Dressage test sheets may be obtained from the official dressage group for each country; each test is comprised of a series of interrelated movements, which are progressively more difficult as the tests get harder. However, at the lower levels a dressage test will involve simple movements only, and the judges will be looking for a well presented combination of rhythm and obedience, the horse moving smoothly away from the leg and staying soft in his way of going.

Dressage to music is becoming increasingly popular, and classes

Not a 'pure' dressage horse by any means, but obviously listening to his rider, halting square and remaining soft and obedient – even though he looks fit to gallop!

are held at shows and events throughout the year. These classes are often regarded as more fun, as the tests are freestyle, the rider selecting his own music to fit the character and rhythm of his horse. In fact this takes hours of research and listening to different tracks, tapes and records to find music which fits the horse's three paces: first the rhythm of each pace must be checked off with a metronome, then music selected which not only fits the rhythm of each pace, but is also in character with the horse – a tinkly jingle might suit a light-footed pony, but not a 17.2hh Hanoverian! The next step is to compile the test, which should only contain movements of the level of the competition: thus a test for a Novice Freestyle to Music must not contain shoulder-in, for example, which is a movement of Elementary standard. A further complication is that as from 1997, competitors must obtain permission of copyright for all the music they wish to use on a tape – a requirement which for the less dedicated makes compiling such a tape even more complicated. Riders are advised to contact their relevant official dressage group for advice.

Problems in the arena

SOLUTION The horse must be walked around in a quiet area and then asked to concentrate on easy movements such as transitions or school figures. These will help to supple up the muscles, which in turn will improve the horse's rhythm. If he begins to stiffen up in the head or neck, the rider should try to work him long and low, encouraging stretching of the neck and jaw. If there is no time to do this before going into the arena, the rider must make sure he carries out the test with a very still, light contact, as the horse will become stiffer if he fights against a heavy hand.

If the horse misbehaves in the ring – bucks, shies or steps out of the arena – accept what has happened and continue calmly. The horse must be driven forward with a strong leg, and not chastised or even spoken to. The rider must stay calm even if he is very disappointed, and continue as best he can. After all, a mistake in one part of the test is not the end of the world!

No matter what goes wrong in the arena, the rider can only do so much; he should work through the problem calmly, and make every effort to ensure it does not happen again. This may be done by schooling carefully at home, and using a bit of forward planning; it might be wise to give the horse calming herbs a few days before the test, and take copious amounts of fly repellent to the event if the conditions are hot and humid.

PROBLEM Having reached the dressage arena, riders may find that their horses do not perform quite as expected. This may be down to rider nerves being transmitted to the horse, or the general excitement of the event. Perhaps the horse has tensed up, which will prevent him from moving fluently and will affect his stride and rhythm. What can you do to help?

The situation every rider fears: a showring tantrum! Think positive: if you go into the ring expecting your horse to play up he is quite likely to pick up on your nervousness and react to it

Main governing bodies

Main governing bodies of other countries who will supply relevant details for societies/associations for the various disciplines:

United Kingdom
Main Governing Body: British Horse Society (BHS), The British Equestrian Centre, Stoneleigh Park, Kenilworth, Warwickshire CV8 2LR, Great Britain
Junior: The Pony Club: as BHS
Showjumping: British Showjumping Association, as BHS
Horse Trials: Horse Trials Group, as BHS
Endurance: The British Horse Society Endurance Riding Group, as BHS
Dressage: Dressage Group, as BHS
British Horse Society Endurance Group: as BHS

Ireland
Main Governing Body: BHS Northern Ireland, House of Sport, Upper Malone Road, Belfast, Co Antrim BT9 5LA. and/or Equestrian Federation of Ireland, Ashton House, Castleknock, Dublin, 15, Ireland.
Show Jumping: The Show Jumping Association of Ireland (N Ireland), 18 Carnalea Road, Castletown, Fintona, Co Tyrone, N Ireland BT78 2HP.
Horse Trials: The Irish Horse Trials Society, Northern Region Management Committee, 12 Bridge Street, Killyleagh, Co Down, BT30 9QN
Dressage: Irish Dressage Society, (N Ireland), 140 Portaferry Road, Newtownards, Co Down, N Ireland, BT22 2AH
Endurance: Irish Long Distance Riding Association, (N Ireland), 188 Ballynahinch Road, Dromore, Co Down, N Ireland, BT25 1EU

Scotland
Main: The British Horse Society Scotland, Wester Gormyre, Torpichen, Bathgate, West Lothian EH48 4NA
Endurance: Scottish Endurance Riding Club, 9 Elliot Road, Jedburgh, Roxburgh, TD8 6HN

Wales
Main: The British Horse Society – Wales, Doldrement, Gwbert Road, Cardigan, Dyfed SA43 1PH

United States
Main Governing Body: American Horse Shows Association, 220 E 42nd Street, 4th Floor, New York, NY10017
Junior: The United States Pony Clubs, 329 South High Street, Westchester, PA 19382
Horse Trials: United States Combined Training Association, 292 Bridge Street, South Hamilton, MA 01982

United States	Dressage: United States Dressage Federation, P.O. Box 80668, Lincoln, NE 68501
Australia	Equestrian Federation of Australia, 52 Kensington Road, Rose Park, SA 5067
New Zealand	New Zealand Equestrian Federation, 121 Queen Street East, P.O. Box 47, Hastings, New Zealand
Canada	Canadian Equestrian Federation, 1600 James Naismith Drive, Suite 501, Gloucester, Ontario K1B 5N4 Canada
France	Fèdèration Français d'Equitation, Rue de Tolbiac 25/27 75013 Paris, France
Germany	Deytsche Reiterliche Vereinigung, Freiherr-von-Langen Strasse 13, PO Box 110 265, 48231 Warendorf, Germany
Belgium	Fèdèration Royale Belge Des Sports ƒquestres, Avenue Houba de Strooper 156 1020 Bruxelles, Belgium
Denmark	Dansk Ride Forbund, Langebjerg 6, 2850 Naerum, Denmark.
Italy	Federazione Italiana Sport Equestri, Viale Tiziano 74, 00196 Rome, Italy

Index